GARDEN OF EAGLES

GARDEN OF EAGLES

The life and times of a falconer

David Fox

Patrick Stephens, Wellingborough

Dedication

To my wife, Jill, who has shared our home with many
large birds of prey and endured incubators, brooders
and clamouring chicks for weeks on end in the privacy
of the bedroom. Also to my long-suffering parents who
encouraged me with my raptor studies from the very
beginning. I owe them all my most grateful thanks, for
without their unceasing co-operation, this book may
never have been written.

First published 1984

British Library Cataloguing in Publication Data

Fox, David Glynne
  A garden of eagles.
  1. Wild birds, Captive
  2. Birds of prey
  I. Title
  636.6'869   SF462.5

  ISBN 0-85059-706-4

Text photoset in 11 on 12 pt Baskerville by Manuset
Limited, Baldock, Herts. Printed in Great Britain on
115 gsm Fineblade coated cartridge, and bound, by
The Garden City Press, Letchworth, Herts, for the
publishers Patrick Stephens Limited, Denington Estate
Wellingborough, Northants, NN8 2QD, England.

Contents

Acknowledgements

The writing of this book would have been very much more difficult without the help of my father, Mr H.L. Fox, who provided many of the early photographs; Alan Reynolds Photographics, Grantham, Lincs; Jim Kershaw of Kershaw Studios, York; the 'Madabout' team of Tyne Tees Television, in particular, Dianne Campbell; and Don Sharp, taxidermist at Wollaton Hall Natural History Museum, Nottingham, who kindly allowed me access to the Whitlock Collection and other egg collections in order to make a photographic study of the entire spread of European birds of prey eggs. Also, my thanks to Frank Olley and Tony Hughes of Nottingham University Photographic Department for prompt reproductions at short notice. For their unfailing encouragement and co-operation, I am extremely grateful.

Foreword by
His Grace the Duke of Rutland

Garden of Eagles is an authoritative and interesting book on falconry and ornithology in Britain, a subject on which many people have little information. The author obviously has great practical knowledge of falconry and has the ability to express his many experiences with clarity and understanding. Everyone who appreciates the countryside and our ancient field sports will welcome this book, which I hope will be particularly instructive to so many of our people who live in an urban environment.

Introduction

Wheeling and soaring high above the limestone massif that forms the beginning of the Pennine Chain in the High Peak District of Derbyshire, floats into view the ornithologically unlikely form of a female Imperial Eagle.

Her real home, before she was taken from her lofty eyrie as a woolly youngster, was the awe-inspiring fastness of the Russian Ural Mountains. But that was more than 14 years ago and since that date she has been making use of somewhat less dramatic slopes which generate the updraughts of air to provide the lift, enabling her broad six-foot span of wing to carry her aloft to a suitable vantage point to search for the prey that is her natural birthright.

I feel privileged to have shared all those 14 years of her life, working as partners, man and bird, sharing a way of life almost as old as the surrounding hills themselves. When she came to me she was wild and savage, full of untamed ferocity, and I am proud to be able to say that, 14 years later, she still retains all these qualities, having lost little, if any, of her affinity with her wild counterpart in her Russian homeland. She is trained but not tamed, her wild spirit always just beneath the surface; yet still we have formed a working relationship which suits both of us.

Out from the shadow of a great rocky buttress, the sun glinting on her golden head and the wind bending her dark brown primary feather tips, she swings into view. She is totally free to go in any direction of her choosing, but she resists the strong urge to return to the wild and instead floats high up over the valley floor where I am walking along, dragging behind me through the lush meadow grass, a lure in the form of a stuffed rabbit skin on a long line, to which is also attached a portion of her daily meal.

Looking up, I see her wings fold almost pear-shaped and, descending with alarming rapidity towards the valley floor, she levels out and seizes the lure with her gnarled and powerful yellow feet. As she pulls at the meat on the lure, I make in to her gradually with a larger, more tempting piece held firmly in my gauntlet. Swallowing the sole remaining morsel left on the lure, she elevates the long, lanceolate feathers on the nape of her neck at my approach. Disgusted with the puny amount of meat on the lure she looks around and finally fixes her steely-eyed gaze on the juicy hunk of rabbit waggling about a few feet from her and still in the firm grip of my gloved left hand. With one final convulsive stab at the lure with her feet she is airborn again for a second or two before alighting on my gauntlet with all the finesse of a bulldozer, transfixing her meal with her heavily armoured feet. I wind up the lure-line and make my way to my parked car. The rabbits have eluded us today, but there will be other days.

This is the noble and ancient art of falconry. An art which has brought me immeasurable amounts of joy and happiness as well as moments of sadness and despair. An art which has taken me to many remote corners of Great Britain and which has been primarily responsible for taking up far more of my allocation of spare time than some would deem necessary or desirable.

For more than 20 years I have shared my home and indeed my life with the winged cats of the air, the birds of prey. And why? Well I hope that *Garden of Eagles* can provide the answer to that question. And I hope that you, the reader, will be able to share in some of the thrills and excitement that over the years these wonderful creatures have given to me, from the frustrating, early years of my childhood, full of disappointment, to the relatively successful flying and captive breeding that is so much a part of my life today.

Although during the past 20 years or so, I have trained and flown a number of different species of birds of prey, including Peregrine, Saker, Lanner and Laggar Falcons, Falconets, tropical accipiters etc., mostly with some degree of success, lack of space does not permit their inclusion here. This book is primarily about the true loves of my life, the eagles. There are today but a handful of falconry enthusiasts who regularly fly eagles and I am proud to be counted among this small but elite band.

I am well aware that a greater number of kills could be entered in the day-book simply by using one of any of the smaller birds of prey (which I sometimes do), but for me the size of the bag is unimportant. For sheer elegance and mastery of the air the large eagles are incomparable. Gliding over the undulating landscape on huge, broad sails, head turning this way and that, seeking out their natural prey is a sight not given to many people. I am indeed fortunate, having witnessed that gripping spectacle countless times, and entirely on account of the noble and ancient art of falconry.

Were it not for the techniques of falconry, I may never have witnessed that most exciting of natural dramas, the hunter pursuing the hunted. The more sentimental among us may not easily accept the fact that one animal has to die to sustain and preserve the life of another, maintaining that it is cruel, and that to become excited at witnessing 'the chase' is tantamount to morbid curiosity.

Man himself can be, and often is, one of the most ruthless predators on earth, although, for the most part, he is happy enough to let someone else kill his Sunday joint for him. I personally have no desire to harm any living creature any more than I would wish to take sweets from a child, but I have to admit to a surge of excitement watching a bird of prey hunt and kill. This is probably a throwback to the days when man hunted to stay alive, and although 'civilised' man no longer *has* to kill each day for his food, the urge nonetheless still remains, albeit dormant in many of us. For a classic example of the hunting instinct in man, one only has to watch the excited expression on the face of an angler when his float begins to bob. And how many of us enjoy a days' fishing?

I suppose it all depends upon where one wishes to draw the line. Cruelty, surely, has to apply entirely to the human race. Humans kill other animals (even each other) merely for the novelty of watching them fall, whereas, almost without exception, no wild animals are guilty of such wanton destruction. In falconry, a bird of prey is not trained to kill, it does that by instinct, but trained to return to the falconer. The falconer himself, more often that not, is a mere spectator, watching his bird perform acts that its ancestors have been performing since before man put his first foot on this earth. The falconer then, in my view, is basically a rather specialised bird-watcher.

This book is intended as my tribute to an outstanding class of birds, the birds of prey and eagles in particular. Long may they grace the skies of our world.

David Glynne Fox
Dunkirk, Nottingham
October 1983

Chapter 1

Winky

Obsession. I believe that to be the only suitable word to describe my intense passion for anything concerning falconry or birds of prey. But why do any of us have these deep-rooted and self-satisfying hobbies, pastimes and ways of life? I have often thought that in my case it might well be worthwhile to have my ancestry geneologically traced for hereditary reasons. Within living memory at least, there are no previous records of any members of my family ever having the remotest interest in the training and flying of eagles, hawks and falcons. Yet I still have the strangest feeling that I am merely a successor in a line of falconers from the dark ages of the past. And I hold this belief if only for the fact that my interest began before I escaped from the confines of my push-chair.

My father, who, incidentally, maintains that he cannot recollect this episode of my early life and refuses to believe that my memory can go back that far, had been giving me some morning air, and during the course of this exercise had rambled beneath an apple tree. Staring vacantly skywards, gooing and gurgling, as was my wont, my infantile gaze met with that of a wild Tawny Owl. My father must have pushed my pram in a circle around the bole of the tree, for the owl's head swivelled in the same direction. I have seen many owls since that day, yet the great brown head of that Tawny Owl, with its huge black eyes, remains as clear in my mind as any recent owls of my acquaintance. If events in due course show that my obsession is not hereditary, then the blame for my rather eccentric way of life must rest at the door of that Tawny Owl.

After that early confrontation, the only raptors that I encountered during my primary school years were either in zoos or picture-books. My main pursuit of those days, which is still strong today, was the collecting and breeding of butterflies and moths. My father had collected them long before I was born and I have always considered myself fortunate in having such understanding parents.

My father was an excellent teacher and he introduced me to many aspects of our varied fauna. The knowledge that I gleaned from him was in due course passed on to the circle of friends I had made at school. We were friends because of our mutual interests which came to the fore after school was done for the day. Then our learning would really begin, or at least, the most interesting

A Tawny Owl. This species may well have begun the author's passion for birds of prey.

part of it. We would descend upon the woods and fields with our nets and collecting boxes and experience some of the happiest moments of our lives.

Towards the end of my primary school education, my younger brother, Bryan, and I had been collecting newts in Johnson's pond, half a mile from our home and situated on the summit of a rise, high above the Mapperley golf course and about four miles west of the Nottingham city centre. At the base of the slope was a large orchard consisting of a number of old apple trees, the only really large group of trees in the immediate area. There were a few massive ash trees dotted here and there among a network of low hawthorn hedges which criss-crossed the golf-course and, to add to the golfers annoyance, a sizeable herd of Friesian cows grazed unconcernedly all over the place.

The newt pond, or Johnson's pond as it was called locally, was a natural one, being fed by an underground stream, the overspill providing for a marsh on the downward slope of the pond which gradually seeped towards the orchard. To one side of the marsh stood the one and only oak tree in the vicinity, and even this was dead, killed by generation upon generation of Lesser Stag Beetles and their wood chewing, burrowing grubs. The heartwood of the tree had long since been turned to dust by the actions of these beetles and what little bark remained, provided day-time shelter for hordes of Heart and

Dart noctuid moths. It was from one of the decaying branches of this tree that Bryan saw what he took to be an owl of some species take wing and glide over the marsh and down into the orchard.

Knowing of my passion for owls and indeed all birds of prey, my brother rapidly informed me of what he had witnessed whereupon, as quickly as I could extricate my gum boots from the muddy bottom of the pond and marsh, made our way into the orchard through a clearing which had been made in the surrounding hedgerow. Having entered the orchard, neither of us could make up our minds which part to search first and in the finish we decided to work our way down through the trees from the highest ground. As it happened, this decision saved us a great deal of time, for within minutes, Bryan had spotted the bird again, at roost in an apple tree at the very edge of the orchard. We needed no binoculars to help us identify the bird as a Little Owl, the very first either of us had ever seen. Our sudden breathless arrival beneath its tree must have disturbed the owl for it vacated the branch and we had a fleeting glimpse of it as it manoeuvred through the trees, followed by several blackbirds, which, along with many other song-birds, always mob predatory birds whenever they expose themselves. Although it had cost us our newts, we felt it was more than worthwhile to be able to observe such a bird in its natural habitat.

As the summer of that year wore on, a school friend acquired a nestling, or eyas, Little Owl, but insisted on keeping the whereabouts of the nest to himself. It was a beautiful little bird and my heart ached for one like it, not realising at that tender age that it was illegal to remove the eggs or nestlings of protected birds under the 1954 Protection of Birds Act, without a licence from the Home Office.

However, in those days, birds of prey were considered by the vast majority to be nothing other than vermin and as such the only expense incurred in their direction would have been a charge of buckshot. The law was seldom, if ever, enforced, unlike today where, ironically, the birds of prey have become symbols for the conservationist movement and have raised their status, quite rightly, from that of vermin, fit only for the gibbet, to that of a highly beneficial order to be afforded special protection from would-be marauders, including falconers.

The irony is that, since time immemorial, falconers have campaigned for the protection of the birds of prey, albeit for a selfish reason. In point of fact, during the mediaeval period in England, penalties were levied upon offenders who were found in possession of hawks which were not theirs by right of law. Falconry was taken very seriously by most of our reigning monarchs, each one laying down various rules and regulations appertaining to the use of such birds, and woe betide such of their subjects who would dare abuse them.

Since the seventh century then, falconers are the only body to have striven for the protection and survival of the tools of their trade and it seems to me most unfortunate that falconers are receiving much blame for the decline of birds of prey on a global scale. The opponents of falconry have, through the media and elsewhere, managed to convince the public at large that the sport is threatening the existence of our raptors through the 'recreational use of wildlife', and at the same time neglecting to mention that shooting interests, encroachment and destruction of natural habitat, land drainage and flooding for the construction of reservoirs, agricultural poisons and pesticides and natural predation, to mention but a few, are hazards far more serious to the existence of raptor species than all the falconers put together. Bona-fide falconers would rather release their stock to the wild than steal it.

Suffice it to say that the sight of my friends owl drove me once more to Johnson's orchard where we had sighted the Little Owl during the early summer. Maybe, I hoped, the bird had paired up and nested and with a lot of luck, I might be able to find it and obtain a nestling of my own.

I climbed many trees investigating likely looking holes, but, with the exception of the odd apple, the search proved fruitless. After a couple of hours of hopeless hunting I was bent on calling it a day, when a Blue Tit, in an apparently agitated mood, screamed abuse at me from the lofty boughs of an ancient, gnarled apple tree. I knew that she had a nest in a hollow branch in the topmost section of the tree and that she also had several small, rufous-spotted white eggs in it the last time I paid her a visit, but judging by her attentions towards me I assumed that they must have hatched.

I remained at the foot of the tree for a few moments and watched the tiny bird fly away. As soon as she was out of sight, I climbed the tree and peeped into the nesting hole. The young had certainly hatched, in fact the whole nest seemed to be filled with little gaping red maws, each one eagerly waiting to be crammed full of insects. They were well feathered and not so much different from their parents, with the exception that they were more of a yellowish hue.

The adult bird returned and was perched on one of the outermost twigs, chittering defiance at me. Having no desire to cause her any further upset, I began my descent of the tree. Upon placing my foot on a cracked branch to provide some extra support, I spotted a pair of black and yellow eyes staring up at me, watching my every move through a crack in the bark. My whole body quivered with excitement, for as I moved out onto the branch I was rewarded with a sharp clopping sound. I almost fell out of the tree with ecstacy, for at long last, I had found my owl.

Scrambling back into position, I peered into the crevice. The owl suddenly came to 'life' and struggled to get further up inside of the hollow branch. The further the owl struggled, the narrower the branch became, and it soon became apparent that I had unwittingly caused the bird to get itself stuck fast, so that now it was trapped unless I could do something to help it. I discovered the original nest-site down in the trunk of the tree and it was obvious that the owl had ventured up the hollow interior until it discovered this branch leading off from the main trunk. For probably the first time in my young life, I temporarily forgot my long urge to own a raptorial bird and concentrated my thoughts on trying to save the wretched creature from the miserable death of starvation. But to extricate the owl from its desperate position I needed tools. I tried to widen the mouth of the branch with my small pocket knife, but that was virtually useless. Then I remembered an old tenon saw that I had seen a few days previously on a nearby rubbish dump. The tip was some half a mile

A Little Owl

distant and I ran at top speed all the way, arriving on the scene in an exhausted state. Then, to my utter dismay, I found that some helpful person had dumped a mountain of garden refuse directly above the spot where I knew the saw lay. I dug and rooted beneath the wall-flowers and other garden throw-outs for several minutes, finding a pair of rubber washing-up gloves on the way down. These, I considered, might come in useful when handling the owl, for I was not over-enthusiastic about having my hands raked apart by its sharp talons.

After locating the rusty old saw, I rushed back to the orchard to remedy the owl's plight. By the time I reached the tree the sun was at its highest peak and I sank down upon the grass in the shade, wheezing for breath and croaking like a frog. I remembered the owl's dilemma and swarmed up the tree-trunk. I managed to sit myself safely astride the branch and began to saw a foot or so to the rear of the bird, trying hard not to frighten it any more than necessary. As the blade began to bite into the bark there came an audible 'ping', and I watched helplessly as the broken half of the saw blade bounced its way down among the branches to the grass below. Luckily, there were enough teeth left on the saw to render the continuance of my efforts worthwhile and I succeeded in sawing about half-way through the branch when I decided to stop for a rest. I made an attempt to break off the portion containing the owl, but it was a stalwart branch and it resisted my efforts.

What I did not realise was that while I had been sawing, the owl had struggled in fright and was at the mouth of the hollow branch. Cupping my hands around the entrance to the hole and lying prostrate along the branch, I managed to get into a sort of semi-comfortable position and waited for a few moments until I felt the owl roll out into the palms of my hands. He sat there for a few moments, blinking in the afternoon sunshine and then suddenly dug both sets of sharp little talons deep into one of my fingers and followed up by biting aggressively into my thumb. There's gratitude for you!

He closely resembled the adult Little Owl that we had seen earlier except for the fluffy down feathers on his head and wings. As I stood amongst the trees with the owl on my hand, I began to wonder what on earth my parents were going to say when I arrived home with my pride and joy. After all, I thought, he wouldn't need continuous feeding with insects like the baby Sand Martins that I hand-reared during the previous summer holidays. They ate more than their own weight in insects daily and I wasn't really sorry when they eventually flew away. My father is a very keen naturalist in many fields and who gave me many a lecture against bringing home various waifs and strays, especially 'lost' fledgling birds, emphasising that their parents were seldom very far away and were better left where they were. I know now of course that he was absolutely right, but at that age I failed to see his point of view, and to me, it seemed the birds were homeless and felt it my duty to care for them until they were fit enough to be released. My problem now was to face my father's views on the owl.

My father was serving as Sergeant-Major with the Sherwood Foresters Territorials and was just about to go off on a weekend camp when I arrived home, green with algae, grazed arms, torn shirt and bleeding fingers. I need not have been so concerned, for my father was well aware that owls were far easier to keep than small insectivorous birds and therefore gave me permission to keep the little bundle of fluff. In fact, he went a stage further. Before going off to camp he made a cage for my new-found pet. He dug out an old aquarium of considerable size in which we used to keep a varied assortment of tropical fish. The glass had long since been removed and my father covered the framework with wood and wire-mesh. As soon as it was completed, the cage was fixed to the outside wall of our house in an area that was free from draughts and was not exposed to the harsh weather of the winter months. With the construction now finished, my father went off to camp, leaving me with another problem: food for the owl. As it was Sunday, all the local butchers were closed, ruling out that source. Consequently, I decided that his first meal with me would have to consist of lesser fare and that insects would have to fill the bill. Actually, this was not as drastic as it sounds, for Little Owls are largely insectivorous, and I recalled seeing a photograph of one feeding on a large earthworm.

I went indoors and a short while later, emerged with a metal box in which to collect some insects. After roping in some friends to give me a helping hand, we set off on our insect safari down the avenue where we lived. The avenue was privately owned and totally unmade with most of the hedges well over-grown. Frequently, all the local children, myself included, were enlisted to help dig out lorries and cars which had become stuck fast in mud. Towards the bottom, the avenue petered out in, or rather merged with, several orchards. It was therefore a natural haven for a varied collection of flora and fauna.

We must have looked a peculiar sight, hosts of kids with their heads thrust into the hedgebottoms, behinds skywards, grabbing anything which ran on six

His eyes lit up at the sight of a centipede.

or more legs. I came upon some old, damp and mildewed sacking, and beneath this I found enough crawling food to sustain my owl for a week. I filled the box with earthworms, centipedes, millipedes and several Violet Ground Beetles. Some of my friends had found other creatures including a large Dor Beetle, and all of these were ceremoniously emptied into my tin.

On arrival home I dashed to the cage on the wall to see if the owl was still all right. He was gazing at a saucer that had been placed on the floor of his new home. We had a cat at the time, a huge Persian tabby that was reminiscent of a Scottish wild cat, and my mother, knowing that I had no food for the owl, had placed a saucer-full of tinned cat food in the cage for him. I removed the saucer, but felt very smug that my mother too was taking an interest in the welfare of my bird. The owl's eyes lit up at the sight of a centipede wriggling between my fingers and he snapped at it, my fingers included, then stood splay-footed with the squirming creature in his beak. He ran to a corner of his cage and swallowed the beast whole. I then placed the Dor Beetle on the cage floor and retired several feet to watch the events. As the purplish-black beetle crawled over the woodwork, I observed that the owl never once took his eyes off it. His head swivelled corkscrew-like through what seemed like an impossible degree until he finally struck the beetle with one of his feet and threw it across the cage in apparent disgust. Seconds later, he again grabbed it with one foot and this time transferred it to his beak, splitting open the beetle's wing-cases, or elytra, and commenced to rip it to shreds. I placed one or two worms and a few insects into a circular tin which was fitted with an overhanging lip to prevent them from crawling out. When I left, the owl was standing on the edge of the tin with his head buried inside, busily sorting out the tastiest morsels. He was already beginning to settle down in his new environment.

After a couple of days, I decided the next step would be to handle him and find out just how tame, if at all, he really was. I donned the rubber gloves that I had found on the tip and opened the cage door to get him out. After his settling-in period he was full of fight and ready for anything and anyone. Throwing himself on to his back he presented both sets of talons ready to transfix me. Cautiously, I put my hand towards him and he followed up by stabbing at the glove with both feet, ripping the rubber at the finger-tips to shreds. I left him to calm down for a minute or two while I discarded the remains of the glove, and then, bare-handed, I tried again and succeeded in obtaining a hold on one of his feet, while he succeeded in getting a hold between my thumb and forefinger with his beak. While still in this uncomfortable position, I carried him indoors and upstairs into my bedroom where I closed the door and fastened all the window catches. The idea of this exercise was to observe his capabilities of flight, or lack of them.

It was a relief to turn him loose for my blood was beginning to flow quite freely. He circled the room several times and eventually collided with the curtains where he remained, bat-like, for several moments before releasing his grip and alighting on the window-sill, panting with exertion. I left him to recollect his wits while I paid a visit to the local butcher and bought two pieces of fresh rabbit meat, which I dissected into small portions and added liberal amounts of fur and bone particles. Owls, unlike diurnal birds of prey, have no crop in which to store their food prior to digestion and their prey,

Owl pellet, or casting, dissected, showing bone and fur remains.

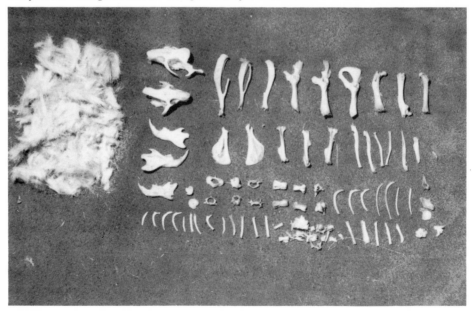

usually mice, shrews, voles and small birds are generally swallowed whole. The bones, fur and other indigestable matter being regurgitated through the mouth, or beak, a few hours later, usually early the following morning. This casting, or pellet, varies in size and shape in accordance with the size of the bird in question and the intake of roughage at the previous feed. All predatory birds regurgitate these castings, as do many other species of birds and much can be learnt from them.

Most of the old-time gamekeepers and also, unfortunately, too many of the modern ones, have left the bulk of the blame for the sudden demise of their pheasant and other game poults at the door of avian raptor depredation and have a marked tendency to shoot or trap on sight, anything with a hooked beak. Admittedly, given the opportunity, some hawks will raid the rearing pens rather than do an honest days hunting for natural quarry but, generally speaking, raptorial birds are largely beneficial to mankind. The Tawny Owl, for example, is known to be among the greatest of rat hunters, yet they are still to be seen hanging on some gamekeepers' gibbets. Toxic insecticides, overhead pylon cables, inclement weather, stoats, weasels and other four-footed predators are responsible for reducing gamebird numbers in far greater quantities than all the birds of prey put together. If regular examinations were made of the birds' castings from daytime perches or roosting places, it would soon be apparent whether or not the bird was the guilty offender. Not so long ago, the Little Owl was heavily persecuted because it was widely believed to be responsible for committing mass depredations upon partridge chicks, but recent examinations of its castings have largely dispelled this theory and show that the bird is mainly insectivorous, varying its diet with small rodents and the occasional small bird.

The roughage which I added to my owl's meat would replace that which he would have obtained naturally in the wild state. Roughage serves a useful purpose by cleansing the slimy mucus from the digestive tract and, if the castings are found to be of an abnormally slimy texture, it generally follows that either the bird requires more roughage or could be suffering from some malady. Therefore, the state of the castings can be a fair guide as to the health of the hawk or owl.

After a week or so, my owl was beginning to show some signs of calming down, so I gave him a second trial flight in our spare room. He rapidly learned to evade corners and other obstacles in the room and on two or three occasions he actually alighted on my head or shoulders. One afternoon, I left the owl alone in the spare room while I went for afternoon tea. Upon my return I was horrified to find hundreds of pheasant feathers strewn all over the floor. I had a stuffed cock pheasant in an opened case (the glass had been removed years previously) that was kept in one corner of the room and the owl had found it. He popped up his mottled head from somewhere in the interior of the stuffed bird and for some unknown reason be began to put on a display of apparent innocence, possibly to try and make me believe that he had absolutely nothing to do with it, for he came running out and flew onto my shoulder and gave me a friendly nip on my ear-lobe.

I had never noticed such behaviour in him before and I hope that I may be excused for thinking that this was his way of trying to pacify me if he thought that he had brought about my wrath. Of course, he had most likely mistaken the pheasant for food, but either way, he looked so comical in his attempts to make up for his wrong doings that I could only forgive him, and began to clean up the mess he had made before my parents saw it and banned him from the house. Besides, I believe a live owl has far more desirable qualities than a stuffed pheasant. The latter had to be thrown away for it was completely ruined.

Feeding the owl by hand was often painful, as he would snap up my fingers as well as the food. This problem was overcome by placing a small piece of meat on a stick or, in our case, a long-bow arrow with the head sawn off. While taking the food from this stick, he would wink one or the other of his eyes and, because he also performed this habit at frequent intervals throughout the day-time, my mother suggested that we ought to call him 'Winky', and so Winky he became.

In a comparatively short period of time, Winky became very tame, and before long I could trust him loose indoors or out. He did not seem to want to fly away. One afternoon, he came in from one of his rampages outside and flew on to one of the arms of our settee. Our cat, and his brother from next-door, Sparky, just happened to be dozing on the settee after their mid-day meal when Sparky sleepily swiped at Winky with his paw. Although the blow missed its mark it was obvious that Winky had taken a dislike towards these offensive creatures, for he flew straight at the piebald cat and dug his talons deep into his face, taking a small chunk out of his nose. The animal screamed in terror and half ran, half flew out of the back door.

Our own cat was still half asleep when the enraged Winky grabbed him by one of his hind-legs. He too jumped up at this assault upon his peace and tranquility and sought refuge behind the settee. Poor Tibby. Winky flew back onto 'his' arm of the settee where he stood in triumph, his feathers still bristling with anger. I am sure that had he been capable, he would have beaten his wings against his breast in true Tarzan-style. As for Sparky, he carried the scar on his nose for the remainder of his days, serving no doubt as a grim reminder that small owls are better left to their own devices, for I never again saw the cats in close proximity while Winky was on the loose. I had witnessed the fight from behind the half-open kitchen door, ready to separate them in case Winky came off second best, but my fears were unfounded, Winky had won his spurs in the 'pecking order' of the family and proved that he could more than take care of himself.

On one of his first major flights into the outside world he performed several circuits around our house, some 300 feet in circumference. The neighbours thought that I had lost him for good, and indeed it seemed that way but, before long, and much to my surprise, he flew back to his cage and vanished inside. Possibly the sheer size of the green world outside may have unsettled him, for he was still very young. At this stage in my 'career' I hadn't a clue how to make jesses, the leather straps which are cleverly fitted around a hawks' legs to render the handling of the bird a less cumbersome task and also alleviates the stress caused by handling bodily. But because of Winky's placid temperament I really had no need for jesses.

The summer was drawing to a close when one morning, my friend who owned the other owl came to see my bird. As a result, finding that we probably had a pair between us, (my friend's owl was larger than mine so we assumed it to be a female, females being larger than males in the majority of birds of prey) a plan was hatched so that we could put them together in an attempt to breed from them. I considered this to be an excellent idea and on account of my friend's owl being still very wild through being kept loose in a spacious shed and seldom handled, I thought it would be preferable to introduce my owl to his. I transported Winky to my friend's house in a travelling cage that had originally been made for finches, and then introduced him to what we hoped would be his new mate. No fighting broke out and both birds appeared to be interested in each other, so we left them side by side, perched among the rafters and beams.

The school holidays came to a close all too soon and it was back to school on the Monday. My friend and I attended the same school and so I decided to call for him on the way, so giving me an opportunity to find out if the owls were still in good health. On arrival at the back door of my friend's house, I glanced down the crazy-paved garden path towards the shed. I stared into the pear trees spreading their fruit-laden branches above the shed roof and then gazed along the top of the high brick wall which enclosed the garden on three of its sides. It was then that my heart missed a beat, for there, perched on the wall, was a Little Owl. I knew instantly that it was Winky and I ran down the garden path to try and coax him to come down to me like he always had done. But all that had changed now. He didn't seem to want to know me. The other owl called to him from somewhere in the midst of a pear tree, and turning, he flew up to join her. He had forgotten all about me. I felt as though the bottom of my world had fallen through.

The two owls flew in harmony into a group of aged willows and were lost to view forever. Stricken with grief, I wended my way to school alone, seeking only my own companionship and straining to hold back the tears now welling up in my eyes. Throughout the day I could not concentrate on my schoolwork, my thoughts were only on Winky and of the many happy hours that we had spent together. My tears splashed onto my exercise books as I stared vacantly out of the classroom window to the green fields beyond, remembering and reliving events of the past months. But despite my sad loss, I made a vow that fateful day, little realising at the time that destiny would place many avian raptors my way, that one day, somehow, I would own another bird of prey. I learned some time afterwards that my friend's uncle had accidentally left the shed door ajar, allowing the birds to escape. It was probably all for the best and I can but hope that they settled down somewhere and reared a family or two. I have visited Johnson's orchard many times since and amongst the numerous birds seen, I occasionally catch a brief glimpse of a Little Owl. I like to think that it is Winky, or one of his progeny.

Chapter 2

Trials and tribulations

I gradually overcame my grief at the loss of Winky, but the stage was set and I began to concentrate all my efforts on acquiring a replacement for him. I knew of no one who could help me in my quest and knew of no establishment where such birds could be bought, so it seemed that the only solution would be to try and catch another. Shortly after losing Winky, my parents moved house and we came to live in neighbouring Carlton, which, like Mapperley, is a suburb on the outskirts of Nottingham. The fields in which I had practically grown up, and loved so much, were still within easy access, and I also found new areas where I could search for birds of prey and further my studies of other forms of wildlife.

I was still at school when I came in contact with another breeding pair of owls. These were situated on a cliff-face in the middle of the woods at nearby Colwick. These cliffs, which consist of a mixture of sandstone and red clay, are extremely crumbly and dangerous for would-be climbers and are known to the locals as 'Dead Man's Drop'. A railway line runs along the base of the main cliff and the area is well populated with gigantic ash and sycamore trees. I was walking along the base of this particular cliff one afternoon when, for reasons known only to himself, a small boy asked me if I would like to know the where-abouts of a white owl's nest. I understood him to mean a Barn Owl, although the species is commonly called the White, or Ghost Owl by some country folk. I answered in the affirmative but instead of taking me to the location, as I had anticipated, he simply gave me some instructions to follow.

I must admit that I felt more than a trifle sceptical about the whole affair, but as I had little to lose, I considered it might be worth a try. Following the contours of the cliff for 100 yards or so, I detected a large, rectangular hole, situated about two-thirds of the way up, and according to the boy's story, this was supposed to be the owl's nest. There was certainly an abundance of fresh-looking droppings, or mutes, at the entrance so I climbed a nearby tree to obtain a better view of the nesting site. From even the highest bough I could not see directly into the hole so I turned to begin my descent, when there, perched on the cliff-face just a few feet from my eyes sat a most exquisite example of a male Barn Owl. I knew it to be a male for its breast was unmarked and white as freshly driven snow, whereas a female has a mottled

Dead Man's Drop—Colwick Woods, former Barn Owl haunt. **Above** *Facing south-west.* **Below** *Facing north-east.*

The Barn Owl's eyes were like large black pearls set in a bed of white satin.

breast. Almost as though it were mounted on ball-bearings, its great buff-coloured head swivelled round to gaze at me. Its eyes were remarkably striking, like large black pearls set in a bed of white satin. He took off and flew low over the race-course towards the River Trent like a great moth. I continued my descent of the tree and concealed myself in a clump of elder bushes just below the nesting site to await his return.

He came back some time later carrying prey which, much to my surprise, turned out to be a fish—a small roach. Many owls have been observed taking fish at some time or another but this was the first time that I had personally seen it. The owl alighted at the entrance to the nesting hole, gave one rapid glance in my direction and then vanished inside. I went home with high hopes, full of plans for a return visit the following weekend.

In the meantime, I acquired a rope of dubious quality and 'press-ganged' a few friends for their assistance, all of whom considered that it was bordering on insanity to go over that treacherous drop for a pair of owls that I might not even get. But while I knew that there were owls on that cliff-face, I would not give up easily and despite my friends' protests, I still went through with the venture. Several of them actually joined me, even if it was only for the novelty of watching me fall off the cliff. As we arrived at the base of the cliff, armed with various oddities of climbing paraphernalia, two Barn Owls flew out of a second hole directly above the spot where the little boy had first told me about them. From all points of view, this new site was the most accessible and so it was here that our work began. I anchored the rope, which, with knots here and there, was not in the peak of condition, to a not dissimilar ricketty old fence. My colleagues eyed the rope with grave suspicion and not a one volunteered to test its strength, rightly suggesting that it was my quest and that it was I who would be reaping any rewards. Consequently, I was the first to go down. The drop onto the hard ground below was at least 70 feet and totally sheer, but I considered the venture worthwhile, and so, taking a deep breath and a strong hold on the rope, I slithered over the edge.

The very texture of the cliff made climbing very difficult, for the sandstone gave way whenever I attempted to secure a foothold, and the clay was dry and crumbly and constantly blew into my eyes and mouth. But after what seemed like an eternity, I eventually found myself standing on a narrow ledge outside the entrance to the nesting hole. I began humming to myself to help take my mind off the sheer drop and jagged boulders below. There were many castings on the ledge and on the floor of the hole, but that was the sum total of information that I ever received from that site.

I dissected several castings while standing on the ledge and discovered that the owls were feeding almost exclusively on shrews and short-tailed field voles, plus the odd sparrow here and there. I made another attempt at the original nesting hole some time later, the resulting experiences of which I shall relate at the end of this chapter.

$$* \qquad * \qquad *$$

I had a happy, if not entirely successful life at school and was quite sad when it all came to an end. The prospect of work seemed such a serious affair after all the joviality of school-life, but I soon settled down after becoming a horticultural technician at a research station in Lenton on the other side of the city of Nottingham.

At about the same period, a friend and I were collecting insects in Wollaton Park, a large and attractive deer-park cum golf-course in central Nottingham. Our search brought us to rest beneath a group of yew trees deep inside one of the many stretches of woodland in the park, where I absent-mindedly tapped the bark of one of the trees with the handle of my butterfly net. This action startled a roosting Tawny Owl which promptly flew out over our heads. We pursued it all over the woodland until eventually we lost sight of it amongst the myriad of trees. I found several of its moulted feathers on the ground beneath the yews and also discovered a few castings, which when broken open, revealed many fragments of common Cockchafer Beetles.

I revisited the yews about a week later and took along a couple of friends so that they could have the opportunity of observing their first wild owl. The yews however, were very dense, and I failed to locate the owl for them. I explained that my disturbing actions a week ago must have caused it to move on and we were on the verge of leaving when not one but two Tawny Owls vacated the yews. My friends were overjoyed, as we had some splendid views of the birds.

One of the most fearless owls that it has been my fortune to come across was a Long-Eared Owl on the Forestry Commission lands at Thieves Wood, near Mansfield. The area is blanketed with dense, regimentally planted pine forest, which provides an ideal haunt for the species, and is relieved with paths, or rides as we call them, forming a network throughout the entire forest. It was

A Long Eared Owl.

on one of these rides that I was lucky enough to observe one of these birds at close quarters.

I was busy collecting fungi at the time, for Mycology, the study of fungi, is a long established hobby which I share with my father, and I had spotted a fine example of a deadly fungus, known under the exquisite name of the Destroying Angel *(Amanita virosa)* which was growing just inside a row of sapling pines. As I sauntered over to examine this rather scarce, deathly white fungus, I only half noticed the pale form perched low down in a pine. Only half noticed it, that is, until the pale form hissed and snapped its beak at me. I turned and glared straight into its eyes, which possessed all the colours of the glowing embers of a coal fire, the most brilliant orange imaginable and with contrasting black pupils. The owl returned my rude stare with ever increasing vigour and presented me with her full threat display. Her head was thrust forward with her beak wide open and emitting the most fearful owl language. She erected both 'ear-tufts' and puffed out her body plumage to its fullest extent. In addition to this she spread her wings, showing off all her fine barring and giving the impression that she was twice her normal size. The audacity of the bird was quite remarkable. I took a step nearer and the owl responded by snapping its beak more rapidly than ever, and then, without warning, the immaculate creature took wing and flew off down the sunlit ride, finally disappearing into a maze of distant pines, leaving the now forgotten Destroying Angel and I standing alone once more amongst the trees.

One afternoon, I decided to do some sketching out in the fields at Gedling, on the west bank of the River Trent. I found a sheltered spot out of the wind on a grassy slope which merged with a wood at the base. Beyond the wood, stretching for some distance, were the grim, grey outlines of slag-heaps from the local colliery, which, with a bit of imagination, would make a rather nice 'mountainous' background for my monochrome sketches. The slopes before me were dotted with large clumps of seeding thistles and I did not have long to wait before I had scarlet-faced Goldfinches, together with Greenfinches and Linnets, busily feeding on the seedheads right in front of me as I sat, almost immobile, in my hidey-hole.

I had been sketching for some time before I became aware of a peculiar restlessness coming over the finches; within seconds they were in panic and scattering all over the fields. I was mystified by all this sudden activity and wondered what on earth was happening. The cause of all the fuss came in the form of a pair of low-flying Sparrowhawks which nipped over the hedge bordering my slope and gave chase after any and every available bird in the vicinity. Neither hawk appeared to single out any particular bird, but rather darted after one and then another. The male Sparrowhawk, or Musket (after which the rifle is named), hit a blackbird which chose that inopportune moment to leave the security of his hedgerow and was sent sprawling back into the hedgebottom in a flurry of black feathers. The Musket banked and followed his prey down in a similar manner to that of a falcon, rather than binding to it in true Sparrowhawk fashion. He carried the bird into the wood and was closely followed by the female. In the hedgebottom, only a few black feathers blowing in the wind were all that remained in evidence of the little drama.

I have an uncle residing in Cheshire whom I visit periodically, who is also a keen and able ornithologist and a voluntary warden at Rostherne Mere reserve. A few years back I stayed with him for a week, hoping to locate a pair of Red-Footed Falcons which my Uncle Russ had spotted in the area, but alas, I was not quite that fortunate, although I did manage to observe other wild birds of prey during my stay. Kestrels were in abundance and were frequently seen hovering in the sky, high above the meres. On a couple of occasions the distant forms of Sparrowhawks were seen winging their way across the open fields and over hedges, but my main interest was to attempt to locate as many species of owls in the area as possible. With my uncle being a very able bird-watcher and a superb companion to boot, it follows that I was only too pleased to have his company.

Our first attempt was to be a nocturnal jaunt in the woods, and we were joined on the hunt by my father, brother and my Uncle Alan from Manchester, who is another keen birdwatcher with superhuman eyesight. He is able to detect from so far away birds that the rest of us have difficulty in spotting through powerful binoculars. We often joke about his 'bionic' eyes, but, nonetheless, his exceptional vision is uncanny.

So, with this stalwart body of men we began by following a long, winding stream, known locally as the 'Red Brook' on account of the red clay content of its bed. This stream ran through the entire length of Bluebell Wood and emptied itself into a large stretch of marshland. The trees were more sparse in the marshy area but their trunks were much broader owing to the lack of competition from other vegetation. There were clumps of Reed Mace, Marsh Marigold and the strange Balsam, or Touch-Me-Not, growing in profusion in the hollows where patches of water collected to form pools, the bright yellow flowers of the marigolds and the orchid-like flowers of the pink balsam could be seen quite plainly in the bright moonlight. The only blur on the landscape was a low, clinging mist which rolled over and played with the ripples on the surface of the Red Brook. All was still and quiet, but every now and then we heard the faint 'plop' of a water vole as it plunged into the crystal-clear waters of the brook.

Half way through the marsh we halted, keeping as silent as the night itself, scanning the area and scrutinising every tree. One member of the party—if I remember correctly, the bionic-eyed Uncle Alan—had detected an odd-looking 'bump' on the bough of a tree across the marsh from us. The moon sent beams of light radiating through the branches, but it was still too dark to make out any important details. The 'bump' came to life and flew across the clearing back to Bluebell Wood. We could tell by its large, rounded silhouette against the sky that it was a Tawny Owl. The bird had been using the tree regularly, as there were numerous castings on the ground. We heard a couple of Tawny Owls calling from various wooded areas, but neither saw nor heard any other species that night.

The following day we did the same run, only this time we approached from the opposite end. One of my uncles, who was leading the party, came face to face with an adult Long-Eared Owl perched upon a fallen log. Both owl and uncle stared at each other in surprise, although the owl recovered from the shock first and flapped off slowly across the clearing. Almost immediately, a soft call from my Uncle Russ at the rear of the party attracted my attention. He had spotted another owl amongst the leafy boughs of an oak tree.

I was much shorter than my uncle, who is well over six feet in his socks, and consequently, I had an inferior view, so to remedy the situation, I decided to climb up part of the tree for a closer look. I had barely set foot on the bole of the trunk when an immature Little Owl flew shakily out. A strong wind had sprung up and the bird was experiencing some difficulty in remaining airborn. I at once had designs on securing it and ran across the fields as fast as my legs would carry me, but it was blown down into a potato field and I never saw it again. Little Owls are well adapted for running along the ground and I believe that it must have run down one of the deep furrows.

Spurred on by this near miss, I went to Wollaton Park shortly after my return from Cheshire. Being the right time of year, I hoped that I might be able to find a fledgling Tawny Owl if the birds had bred at all. I searched their territory from beginning to end with no success and was almost back at the clump of yew trees when I saw one of the owls fly up into a tall beech tree with a rodent of some description held in its beak. From where I was standing it appeared that the owl was depositing its prey into a hollow inside the trunk. As the bird left rather hurriedly, I assumed that the nest was situated there and that the young were old enough to swallow their food without assistance.

It was a stiff climb up the branchless, vertical trunk to a height of about 30 feet, but I considered it was worthwhile, for I was fully expecting to obtain another owl at long last. But alas, as I might well have guessed, good fortune of that kind was out of fashion as far as I was concerned. The hollow was simply one of the owl's food stores as there were several beetles and rodents.

Owls stagger their brood. That is to say, they begin incubation with the laying of the first egg, and there may be intervals of two or three days between the laying of each egg. Consequently, a nest may contain young from the egg-stage to half-fledged. Prey of all types may be used as food, depending on the species, but for the younger owls of the brood, insects will, to a certain extent, satisfy their hunger, whereas mice and other rodents will be required to support the bulk of the older birds. Mice are not always readily available in large enough quantities as would be necessary to satisfy the appetites of a nestful of young owls all of the same age, hence the need for staggering. In this manner, the parent birds have a greater variety of food to choose from and prey in any surplus quantity is often stored during the breeding season to supply their needs in lean times.

I felt like forgetting all about birds of prey and trying something a little less exasperating, like stamp collecting. All these constant failures were doing little to raise my morale and it appeared that my objective was getting more and more futile as time wore on. Every summer, according to newspaper articles, many people throughout the country had found owls, seemingly abandoned by the parent birds in most unexpected places, such as suburban roads and

A Tawny Owl, one of several species which cache surplus food.

gardens; one was even found on a doorstep! They were almost always found by people who didn't really want them, knew even less about keeping them and in a few cases, didn't even know that they were owls! I wrote to some of these people but with negative results. They had given them to a birdwatcher or handed them over to the RSPCA. Yet here was I, searching hard for years on end, in many cases risking life and limb on a cliff-face or up in the crown of some huge tree with not even the remotest success. I was certainly at the back end of the queue when luck was being handed out.

However, during this frustrating period, I did have one very pleasant experience. It was during a very bitter winter of severe snowfalls which lingered on well into spring. Much of the British wildlife had paid a heavy price for that winter, for I found the remains of scores of Fieldfares and Redwings which had given up the struggle of trying to scratch a living from the rock-hard ground and had either frozen or starved to death. The ice-bound land had killed off many insects and birds alike and had all but wiped out the spectacular Kingfisher on account of the fact that most of its haunts were frozen over for long periods, keeping the small fish well out of its reach. A Mute Swan had become stuck fast in the ice at Wollaton Park lake and despite being heavily pecked and buffeted by its huge white wings, a friend and I managed to free it by chopping away the solid ice encasing the bird's feet, after which the ungrateful beast hissed and chased us off across the ice-covered water. Our feet and hands were frozen so we decided to warm up a bit by visiting the hall itself. Wollaton Hall is now a natural history museum, so at least we could have an interesting walk round while we were thawing out. We met another school chum who had also braved the arctic conditions and was spending the day there, and he told us that he had just seen a man standing outside the front of the museum holding a falcon. The words were scarcely out of his mouth when I left them at speed. I was almost at the front of the museum when I first saw the man, but the bird he had perched upon his shoulder was no falcon, it was in fact an immature male Golden Eagle.

The falconer turned out to be a fiery-haired, bearded Scot, who was at that time taxidermist to Wollaton Hall. He was a heavily built man who, in my opinion, really looked the part of a falconer, especially with his ample beard. There were fewer people around the back of the hall and the falconer took the bird there to fly it, inviting me to join him. By this time I had forgotten all about my frozen feet and blue hands and jumped at the opportunity. The falconer, or austringer, to give the correct title to one who flies hawks or eagles as opposed to true falcons, wore a thick leather gauntlet, on his left hand and carried a good length of leather leash which was attached to the jesses by means of a swivel. The eagle's cere, the wax-like portion at the base of the beak which houses the nostrils, and also its feet, were a rich yellow. Its talons were large and black and polished like ebony. The plumage was a dark brown and the long and pointed hackles on its nape, which rippled down to the shoulders, were of a paler shade than the remainder of the body. The huge bird glared at me with a glint in its warm brown, but fierce eyes, sending shivers of excitement through my frame. During the hour or so that I was talking to him, the falconer told me something of the eagle's history. He had purchased it from Spain and had been in his possession for about a year when I met him.

The time came to feed the bird and this was a breathtaking display. He placed the eagle on a wall and walked away, playing out a much longer leash, known as a creance, behind him. At a distance of roughly 15 yards from the bird, the falconer turned to face his regal charge. I remained beside the eagle as though transfixed, hardly able to take my eyes off its sheer size and beauty. The falconer then produced a rabbit's hindleg and held it in his gloved fist, waving it about to attract the bird's attention. The eagle did not appear to be the slightest bit interested in the proceedings and kept up this lethargic behaviour for several minutes, showing more concern for the starlings that were walking about and probing the grass on the lawn.

The falconer repeated the entire operation, only this time from a different wall. This seemed to make all the difference, possibly because I was not now standing next to the eagle, distracting it with my rude stare. Suddenly, it launched itself into the air and glided on to the falconer's outstretched fist, where it started to tear the rabbit to pieces. I had watched many birds in flight prior to this, but none were even comparable with the grace and elegance of this Golden Eagle. As it flew across the lawn towards the falconer's fist, its wings hardly seemed to move, only the emarginated primary feathers at the tips of the wings, resembling somewhat the fingers of a man's hand, were fluttering and bending with the wind. Evening was drawing near and I reluctantly made my way home, leaving the falconer still feeding his splendid Golden Eagle.

After this, I was more determined than ever to obtain some sort of predatory bird. Ever since Winky, the urge had been in my blood, but now it was becoming an obsession. I could never see myself flying an eagle, even if I could get one, so I considered that it was time for another attempt to secure one of the Colwick Barn Owls. First of all, however, I thought that a reconnaissance of the site would probably be of advantage. On my arrival, one of the owls left the cliff and vanished into the midst of a group of ash trees, so I climbed the tree close to the nest-site, hoping for a second glimpse of it. The remaining owl, 'came out of the sun' in classic Battle of Britain fashion, resented my intrusion and informed me so in no uncertain terms by clouting the back of my head with its taloned feet. With concentrating my observations on the ash trees and standing awkwardly on a narrow branch, I was not in the most favourable of positions to withstand such an attack and was sent hurtling out of the tree forthwith. Fortunately for me, my fall was broken by a coarse hawthorn bush, and apart from a thousand stab wounds from the thorns, the only other injuries that I sustained were a few small cuts and bruises. From that point on, I treated the Barn Owls with a shade more respect.

On the nights that followed, I was accompanied by two friends, and the first night we began our operations by sitting on the brink of the cliff, pondering a plan of action. Quite by accident, one of my friends happened to kick some loose clay down the cliff-face. This caused one of the owls to fly out from the nesting hole to the ash trees across the void. A second owl followed suit shortly afterwards. The following night we brought into action a set of walkie-talkie radios, so that we could split up but still keep in contact with each other. It was almost dusk and the owls were beginning to sally forth on their nocturnal jaunts. Their peculiar hisses could be heard from a considerable distance and on one or two occasions I heard the true screech, which gives the owl its country name of 'Screech Owl', which is not to be confused with the true Screech Owl, a small American bird belonging to the genus *Otus*.

I walked along the top of the cliff for 50 yards until I almost strode into both owls as they rested on an overhang just in front of me. At the same instant, one of my friends radioed from the far end of the cliff with the message that he had located a Barn Owl in a tree just above him. I radioed back informing him that he must be mistaken, for both owls were in my view, but I had hardly got the words from my lips when a pale, ghostly form in the shape of a fourth Barn Owl alighted between the two in front of me. We located a total of five different Barn Owls, although three of them must have been juveniles that were still lingering around the nest-site. So, they had flown, and I had missed them yet again.

Undaunted, however, I decided I would have one final attempt at securing one. The following week, a friend and I built a tremendous ladder out of railway sleepers and bits of wood that we found in the vicinity of the nest. It took several hours to construct and equally as long to manoeuvre it into position on account of its great bulk, for although it was probably not the largest ladder ever built, it was certainly the heaviest and most cumbersome.

There were two entrances to the nest, one being situated directly above the other, and we had observed the owls using both of them. Neither entrance could have been reached without a ladder as they were situated beneath a large overhang which made descent by rope difficult, if not impossible, for all but the most experienced of mountaineers. I knew from past experience that at least one of the owls had its regular roost there, and I had devised a plan as to how I might trap one. My friend wanted to perform the operation and so, armed with my butterfly net and a non-toxic fumigant, he ascended the ladder. The idea was to place the fumigant in the lower hole and then cover the top hole with the net, hoping that the smoke would force the owl to evacuate the nest and fly into the net. As might be expected, it didn't work out quite as planned. The instant the fumigant was placed in the hole, the owl flew out between my friend's legs and away along the cliff-face before he had the time to even think about the net. I never tried again. They had deserved their freedom and I felt extremely guilty over constantly disturbing them. They had given me many hours of pleasure and I had no desire to drive them away for good, so spoiling future observations.

Some time later, I discovered one of the Colwick Barn Owls dead at the base of the cliff, not far from the nest-site. It had been shot with an air-gun and its wings and feet had been severed and taken as a 'trophy'. I now know that it had been wrong for me, even unforgivable, to have attempted to catch the owls, but I would never have seen them harmed. I could never forgive anyone for such wanton destruction. Had I succeeded in trapping them, they might well have lived much longer in my care, and this tragedy would never have taken place. The remaining owl disappeared after this, and I suspect that this too was probably shot, for I believe that sooner or later, it would have found another mate, as is the way with birds of prey.

However, I was soon to be rewarded for all my trials and tribulations. Raptors were to play a very important role in my life, even if it did mean paying large sums of money for some of them.

Chapter 3

Tentative steps

One day, whilst browsing through the magazines and papers in the local newsagents, I came across a weekly cage-birds' paper in which hundreds of foreign birds were advertised. Among the adverts was one which immediately held rigid my attention, for it stated that several species of birds of prey were up for sale at a Nottinghamshire establishment, and amongst these species were several Pygmy Owls at the modest sum of £3 each. The place was not far from where I lived so I instantly set off to purchase one. At last, after five long years since the loss of Winky, I could go that very afternoon and secure my much sought-after prize. Understandably, my stomach fluttered with impatience and anxiety. I found the establishment easily, which was situated beneath the shadows of an old Saxon church, adding a touch of mediaeval flavour to the scene.

It seemed to me at the time, too incredible for words, and that some unseen powerful force was working against me, for on my arrival I was duly informed that not one, but *all* of the Pygmy Owls had been sold. I considered that after all my previous efforts, I ought to have deserved one by this time. I became even more determined than ever now not to be defeated, so I glanced in turn at all the remaining and, consequently, more expensive stock. These were housed in various sheds and aviaries in the dealer's spacious garden. There were two large wire-mesh flights, in one of which were a pair of Common Buzzards, and in the other was another Common Buzzard and a fine female Marsh Harrier. The main shed contained many other birds including six Kestrels, one immature White-Eyed Buzzard *(Butastur teesa)*, five Besra Sparrowhawks *(Accipiter virgatus)*, one Red-Shouldered Hawk *(Buteo lineatus)* and a similar-looking Broad-Winged Hawk *(Buteo platypterus)*, four Shikra Hawks *(Accipiter badius)* and two Northern Goshawks *(Accipiter gentilis)*. After scrutinising each bird in turn and taking into account the size of my wallet, I finally selected one of the Common Buzzards. I had only been at work for a short period and, not being particularly well off financially, descending from superb, but humble parentage, I could not afford to pay the full cost of the bird outright. I had also still to obtain my father's permission to keep a bird of that size. The dealer who owned the birds required £15 for the buzzard, so I gave him the £3 that I had taken with me for a Pygmy Owl and set about collecting the remainder. In the meantime my beloved buzzard had to remain in its aviary on the dealer's premises.

As expected, my father granted me permission to keep the bird. I sold a Raleigh moped that I had and hardly used and inside a month I was making my final payment on, at long last, a hawk of my very own. The morning that my father and I went to collect the bird was a momentous one for me. I was nervous to the point of bursting with anxiety, which was only relieved when the buzzard was eventually placed into a cardboard box and thrust into my eagerly awaiting arms.

During the period in which I had been paying for the bird, my father and I had constructed a large cage out of wooden export cases that I had purchased from my place of employment, and it was into this cage that I finally turned the enraged buzzard loose. We decided to let her settle down in her new quarters for the night, although I sat and watched her preen and reassemble her ruffled feathers. She puffed out her feathers and slowly pulled one of her feet upwards and then smoothed her breast feathers over it, giving the impression that she was one-legged. She seemed to be settling in nicely.

The following day I was able to make a more detailed inspection of her. Her right eye was slightly smaller than her left and I later found that she was totally blind in it. Her right wing was damaged too. There were no primaries (long flight feathers) in evidence and there were slight trickles of blood oozing from the holes where the feathers had been presumably pulled out. I am not sure to this day of the reason for this, for they rarely grow new ones any faster when pulled and when, and if, they eventually do grow the feathers are often deformed as there is a high chance of damaging the tissues housing them. Fortunately, since that day, I have never seen another case of deliberate feather pulling and I emphasise that it is *not* a practice carried out by falconers.

My buzzard also had a very battered tail and it was plainly obvious that I would be unable to train her for falconry purposes for some considerable time. To the reader, it may seem rather a lot of money to pay for such a cripple, but I was elated with her. It was a waste of time to perform an imping operation upon her, for she was too severely damaged.

Imping is the name of the process where badly damaged or broken flight and tail feathers are repaired so that the hawk can be returned speedily to active service. It is essential that there remains at least a sturdy inch or two of the damaged feather so that a new feather can be grafted (imped) on. For the traditional imping process triangular shaped metal needles are used, pointed at both ends and shaped to fit tightly into the feather shaft. Half the needle is inserted into a new feather of the required size, while the other end is pressed home into the old stump (which is without feeling) using quick-drying glue to ensure a lasting bond. However, years ago I recall seeing a Lanner Falcon (*Falco biarmicus*) which had just undergone a full traditional imping process carried out on both wings. The falcon was placed on its block-perch and the hood removed, whence it sat blinking in the sunshine. As is usual when a hawk has been handled bodily and then placed outside on the weathering lawn, the falcon puffed out its feathers and gave a vigorous rouse, shaking every feather

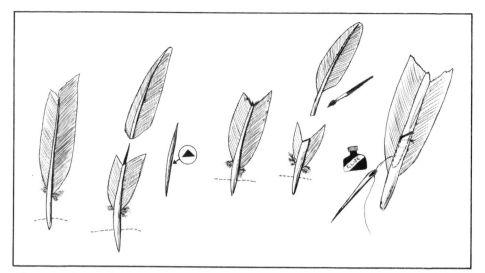

Above *Imping.* **Left** *Traditional method using triangular Imping needle.* **Right** *Imping method using glue and stitching.*

Below *Jappy, my Common Buzzard.*

in its body, causing almost every poorly imped feather to fall out on to the grass beneath the block. This of course meant that the embarrassed and blushing falconer had to repeat the entire operation. Nowadays I use a stitching process which I consider to be more durable and superior to the traditional method. The stump is neatly trimmed and a new feather, with a slightly narrower shaft, is chosen and similarly trimmed. The feathers interlock tightly, one shaft slipping over the other, with two or three stitches passed through and whip-tied to secure permanently.

I had just finished reading the book *Flying Free* by Reidar Brodtkorb, about confined eagles in Norway, and on several instances while observing the habits of my buzzard, she reminded me of one of Mr Brodtkorb's eagles, a Golden Eagle called 'Jappy'. My buzzard was known as Jappy from then onwards.

Jappy, however, was becoming no tamer in the cage, so I consulted a falconry manual and learned how to make and tie on jesses so that I could handle her with some sort of control. I had several sheets of leather that I had bought for the purpose and selected a piece of soft, but strong chrome leather which I cut into two strips, each 9 in long and $\frac{1}{2}$ in wide. The end portion, which was to fit around the hawk's legs, was slightly wider than the remainder of the jess and in this piece I made two small slits along its length, one behind the other and about an inch apart. I also made a third slit at the opposite end of the jess which would later house the swivel. When I had completed both jesses, stretched them and ensured that they were both identical, I rubbed some neats-foot oil into them to render them more supple and impervious to rain.

To fit the jesses, the hawk should first be cast, that is to say, it should be gently, but firmly, held by an assistant and preferably wrapped with a soft, dark cloth to prevent movement, thereby minimising the risk of damage to both falconer and hawk. The widest end of the jess, that is the part bearing the two accurately gauged slits, is wrapped around one leg of the hawk and the tip of this is passed through the second, or rearmost of the two slits. It will be noticed at this stage that if the slits are too far apart, the jess will slip off over the foot, and if too tight, will be difficult, if not impossible, to work through the slit and will impede and may even cut off altogether the circulation of the blood, so causing the foot to swell. Great care must always be taken at this point so as to eliminate any unnecessary suffering. Finally, the other end of the jess containing the single slit is passed through the first slit in the wider end, which should be exposed on one side. The jess is then pulled through to form a neat, non-slip knot. The same applies to the other leg and the task of fitting the jesses is then complete.

A swivel, usually consisting of two brass or stainless steel hoops, riveted together, is fastened to the free ends of the jesses containing the single slits. One free end is passed through one side of the top hoop of the swivel, then the slit is opened and passed *over* the bottom hoop and then pulled up so that it forms an anchorage at the apex of the top hoop. The second jess is passed through in exactly the same way, except that it is poked through the top hoop from the opposite side so that the finished article looks neat and also helps keep the swivel free-running.

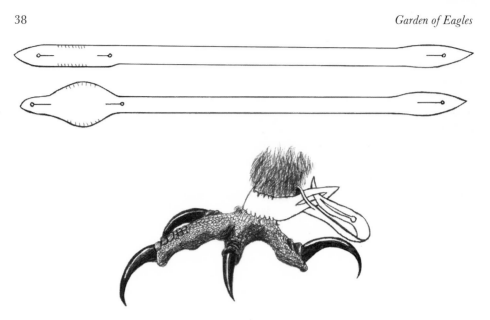

Top *Two types of traditional jesses.* **Above** *Attaching of the jess to tarsi of Golden Eagle.*

Above *Swivels.*

Left *Method of attaching jesses and leash to swivel.*

The leash is now passed through the free bottom hoop of the swivel. This consists of a strip of very strong leather or braided nylon, varying in width according to the diameter of the swivel and the size of the bird in question, a matter of common sense, and is usually about five or six feet in length, tapering to a point at one end. The wide end is then rolled over two or three times, rather like a jam-roll, and a hole is punched into the centre of the roll; the tapered end is threaded through this hole and the remainder of the leash pulled through after it, so forming what is known as the 'button'. This button should be large enough to prevent complete passage of the leash through the lower hoop of the swivel. If sufficient care is taken over the choice of leather and other equipment or furniture, as it should be termed, and is well lubricated, there is no reason as to why it should not last for some considerable time, but I have found that it pays dividends to maintain a regular practice of checking for flaws.

So now my bird was all neat in her jesses, swivel and leash, thanks to the assistance of my father, who held Jappy while I fitted the furniture. The swivel I used came from an old dog-lead, for in those days, falconry had still not made the grade of popularity that it now enjoys and consequently, most equipment was difficult to obtain. Nevertheless, I was ready to begin the lengthy and ever-constant process of manning my buzzard. Manning is merely a term selected from the falconer's delightful jargon meaning to carry a hawk on the glove for daily periods, in order to get it accustomed to strange sights with which it must become well acquainted if it is to be flown with any safety in the field, especially in an urban area. If manning is ignored or neglected, the result could well be a lost hawk. Hawks are, or can be, extremely nervous creatures, so it follows that time spent in manning is seldom wasted, especially at the advent of the bird's career and at feeding times. During the manning period, it is often advantageous to softly talk to and gently stroke the bird, for this sometimes has a calming effect upon its nervous system. It is advisable to use a feather when stroking the bird for two sound reasons. The first is that a nervous hawk is liable to strike the hand and inflict a painful wound with either beak or talons, and the second is that certain oils present in the human skin tend to remove the waterproof bloom that protects the feathers, making them less impervious to rain.

Like most untrained hawks, Jappy bated regularly at first, that is to say, she fluttered wildly from the fist, so much so that she almost drove me to distraction, but I somehow managed to retain my temper and persevered with her. I had read somewhere that if the falconer ever hits his precious charge, as one might a dog, or lets her detect his anger, it would take very much longer (if it became possible at all) before he could do anything with her. Believe me, the temptation to throttle Jappy was just beneath the surface on a number of occasions. And yet, as a direct result of training hawks, I discovered that my own natural fiery temper was gradually being curbed, and I was beginning to become more tolerant of little things in society which would previously have irritated or niggled me.

After bathing her damaged wing, I applied liberal lashings of antiseptic ointment and repeated the performance several times, but improvement was very slight. In desperation, I took her up on my fist and walked to the local PDSA centre, much to the amazement, and I suspect disapproval, of several people who were sitting in the waiting room. They had a variety of pets accompanying them, ranging from a sickly Siamese cat to an egg-bound parrot. One elderly gentleman owned a rather domineering mongrel dog which, up until that point, had been keeping the waiting room in order, but which cowered under a long bench on the far side of the room when it caught sight of Jappy. It must have been the fierce glint in Jappy's eyes that did the trick, for when the surgery began, the patients were only too pleased to push us through the door first.

The veterinary surgeon stated that I should continue to bathe the wing with warm water and to apply plenty of antiseptic ointment. I was assured that there were no broken bones and that the wounds should soon heal, which came as a great relief to me. She regurgitated a casting, or pellet early the following morning. I thought at first that she was attempting to vomit because she held her head downwards, shaking it from side to side and holding her beak wide open. A few moments later, out came the casting, firm, well-shaped and not too moist. At least, her digestive system appeared to be in good order.

Jappy soon became very friendly and acquired a fine glossy sheen on her plumage. She poked her beak into everyone's business and seemed very content with her lot, showing all the signs of making a very fine bird when the time came for her to moult. I was very pleased with her, even though I knew that buzzards were not favourably looked on as being good falconer's birds on account of their lethargic attitude, preferring to feed on small rodents rather than struggle with large rabbits. In more recent years, though, I have seen wild buzzards killing rabbits in both Wales and the Lake District.

With winter setting in rapidly, Jappy spent her nights in our conservatory where she was out of the bitter winds and driving rain and safe from any marauding nocturnal predators, such as foxes, who might find a roosting buzzard easy pickings. I had to spread old newspapers on the floor of the conservatory, for she made an awful mess with her mutes. This I consider to be the only drawback with keeping predatory birds and it can cause much embarrassment to a falconer if his hawk should drop a great white 'trademark' all over someone's expensive fitted carpet or new suit of clothes.

Half-way through the month of January I checked Jappy's damaged wing for fresh feather growth. Bluish quills were showing through and were already over an inch in length. These feathers are known as being 'in the blood' and if they are damaged at this stage, will stream with bright red arterial blood which may result in a deformed feather. I had high hopes that she would be flying in the not too distant future. There was no real need to hold her jesses while handling her in the garden, for I could easily catch her again as she could only flap her one good wing as she ran along the paths. In fact, while I was present in the garden, I allowed her to roam about at will. Her favourite pastime was grubbing about in the hedgebottom after beetles, of which she caught a great many, as inspection of her castings revealed.

Ever since seeing the Golden Eagle at Wollaton Park I had a sneaking desire to emulate the falconer by flying one myself and I had ordered a Tawny Eagle *(Aquila rapax)* from the dealer. I went to visit him one weekend in anticipation that the bird had arrived from India. It was mid-morning when I arrived at the establishment and I considered that if the birds had arrived at all (two were expected) they would most likely be housed in one of the flights. One of the birds was expected to be a Lesser-Spotted Eagle *(Aquila pomerina).*

To my dismay, there were no eagles in the flights, so I peered through the misted window of the main shed. The interior of the shed was rather gloomy and it was dificult to make out any details of importance, but I could just detect two large brown forms sitting in two small cages, or at least I thought the cages were small in comparison with the size of the birds. The cages were stacked one above the other; the bird in the uppermost cage was definitely a Tawny Eagle, but the second bird was darker brown and heavily mottled and streaked with cream. This I took to be the Lesser-Spotted Eagle. The dealer's partner had already laid claim to the Tawny Eagle, I was duly informed, on account of its slightly better plumage, so I had little choice other than to accept the remaining bird. Both eagles were males and I took mine home in the bamboo wickerwork cage in which both birds had travelled the thousands of miles into this country. I spent the afternoon trying to persuade the eagle to perch on my gloved fist out in the garden, but every time I lifted him back on to my glove he would fling himself off again and hang head downwards like a slaughtered fowl. I placed my hand time and time again around his breast to lift him gently back again but each time was rewarded with a dose of furious bating. He had the 'look of the devil' in his eyes and from that moment on I called him 'Satan'.

I battled with him for over four hours before calling it a day and finished up by leaving some food nearby for him. If jessing him had been a simple process, manning looked as though it was going to be quite a drag. I lost count of how many times I lifted him back on to my fist, but I know that my arm felt as though it was dropping off from bearing his weight and the strain of his continuous bating. At this stage in my 'falconry career', I did not properly understand the regular weight check and the complicated restricted diets that are required to bring the hawk into a fit flying condition. I kept on piling the food into him, not realising that I was making a rod for my own back. It was obviously not going to be quite so easy as I had envisaged.

On the very day after I acquired Satan, however, I brought him out of his cage and, much to my surprise, he sat on my glove as though he had been doing it for months. After the previous afternoon's performance I was not expecting much headway for three or four days at least. I gave him some beef to pull at as he sat on my fist and stroked him with one of Jappy's moulted primary feathers. It was a wonderful, almost indescribable, feeling to be handling a real live eagle of my very own which sported a wing-span of almost six feet. These wings were extremely long in comparison with the remainder of his body and when they were spread he appeared to be all wing.

One of the drawbacks with imported birds of prey is that many of them arrive in this country with some defect or another, and Satan was no exception.

Left *Satan, my Tawny Eagle.
Note the sticking plaster on toe.*

Below *He had the look of the
devil in his eyes.*

He had a patch of feathers missing from the top of his head which had probably been caused by constant rubbing on the lid of the box in which he came from India, which was hardly larger than Satan himself. His cere was badly bruised too, but his toes were my biggest headache. One talon had been torn right back to the toe itself, revealing the soft and tender portion known as the 'quick', and every time he stubbed the toe on a rock or suchlike it would start the blood flowing, then out would come the antiseptic ointment. We solved that little problem by binding the talon and toe with a surgical sticking plaster until it had completely healed.

Satan was a dark-fawn-coloured bird with contrasting dark-brown primary and secondary feathers. His tail was dark brown also, with fine greyish-brown bands running horizontally across it. He was a much larger bird than Jappy and twice as fierce, but I was concerned about his weight. I considered 2 lb 12 oz far too low for a bird of his calibre, although with a plentiful supply of good rich meat his breast muscles gradually began to fill out. As he was unacclimatised, I kept him in the conservatory during the winter nights as they were extremely cold that year to say the least.

By this time, Jappy was as steady as a rock on my fist and Satan himself scarcely bated and could be carried about with few problems. In fact, he was almost eager to step on my glove in anticipation of being taken for an outing. His tail was beginning to look a bit scruffy and bent and so, holding him bodily, I dipped his entire tail into a jug of hot water to clean and straighten it out.

It was now evident that Satan was a Tawny Eagle and not a Lesser-Spotted Eagle as I had been led to believe, for both Greater and Lesser-Spotted Eagles have circular shaped nostrils and usually much darker plumage, and although they belong to the same *Aquila* genus as the Tawny, Golden, Wedge-Tailed and Imperial Eagles, etc, the latter have distinctive 'ear-shaped' perforations. Satan's nostrils were definitely ear-shaped and he was far too light in plumage coloration for a Spotted Eagle.

I was beginning to find that all of my spare time was being taken up looking after the two birds. They had to be fed and cleaned out daily and constantly taken out for manning walks, but after all those uneventful years, it was worth it. I had learned step by step how to make jesses and button leashes and so the next step was to learn how to tie the falconer's knot. 'Over, under, round and through', quoted the manual. Two hours later I had mastered it to perfection and woe betide any piece of string I found lying around, for it was soon left hanging upon some obstacle or other, firmly secured by a falconer's knot.

Feeling a mite more confident after this forward move, I went out to face Satan and broke a resolution I had just made. I had resolved, and actually written to the effect in the day-book, that he would not get his food until he jumped on to my fist for it, but I felt so sorry for him when he first looked at the meat and then the ground, then back to the meat, that I left it beside him. In fact I should have reduced his weight gradually now that he was plump and fat with good food, until he became keen enough to overcome his natural fear of man and take the offered food in an acceptable manner.

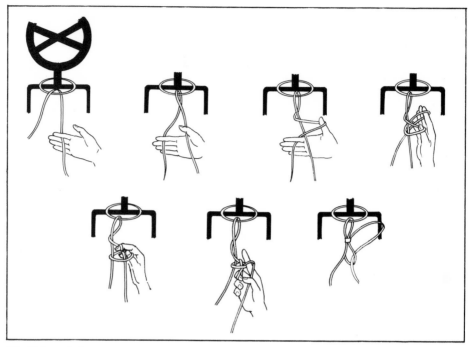

The Falconer's knot.

A hawk should never be starved, for this will rapidly result in loss of fitness and stamina through muscle wastage and any fat reserves will be over-absorbed. I was to learn that this fat reserve is very important when a hawk's weight is being cut down to make it more amenable in the field, rather like an over-weight human athlete who has to diet carefully to give his best performance. While the hawk is being fed on reduced rations, the fat reserves compensate for the reduction in food intake. But the time comes when the fat reserves are all absorbed, and this is the time when the inexperienced falconer comes a cropper and where the weighing machine becomes such a boon. A hawk will lose weight rapidly overnight once the fat has all been absorbed and if the falconer has been weighing his hawk daily, which he certainly should have been, then this sudden drop is soon detected and rectified, by increasing the food intake until the hawk's weight balances with its previous flying weight. Many are the times I have since heard a young falconer say, 'She was flying superbly yesterday, but today she is near death's door', and nine out of ten times the cause is lack of correct conditioning. To enseam, or condition a hawk, takes experience, which can really only be bought with time and careful observation. All trained hawks have a flying weight, that is to say, a weight at which they will perform obediently for the falconer and if brought to this weight at flying times, should give of their best, and are far less likely to be lost than if under or over weight.

Because no two birds are exactly alike, even of the same species and sex, it is difficult, if not impossible, to state outright the exact flying weight for any particular bird. One can at best, only approximate, so the correct flying weight has to be found by experience, trial and error, not necessarily in that order. Even the most inexperienced beginner should soon realise that by daily weighing and monitoring the hawk's subsequent behaviour, he will shortly find the most effective weight-level which results in the highest response for his charge.

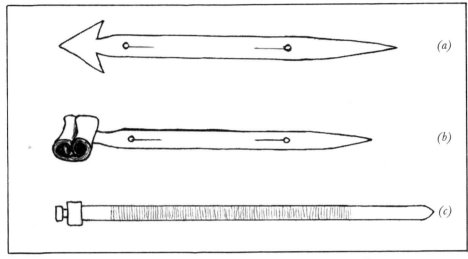

(a)

(b)

(c)

Above *Bewits. (a) Traditional bewit. (b) Button bewit. (c) Plastic cable-tie bewit.*

Below *Hawk Bells. (a) Lahore (Pakistan). (b) Dutch. (c) Asborno 'Acorn Bells', USA.*

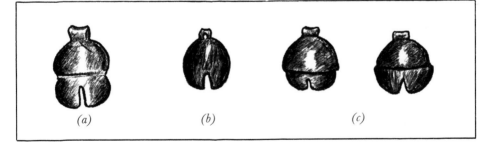

(a)   *(b)*   *(c)*

Left *Aylmeri jess, bell and traditional bewit in-situ.*

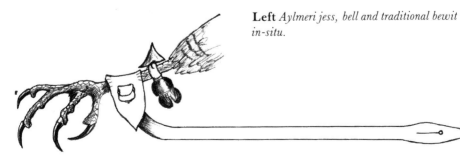

One final word, a hawk should always be flown as high in weight, or condition, as obedience will allow, and if the falconer should err, then let him err in this direction, for it is far easier to strip weight off a hawk than it is to build it up again. A high hawk is a fit and possibly a lost hawk, which is no shame on the part of the falconer, a low hawk is very soon a dead hawk and a black mark.

Now eagles are often a very different proposition. They can prove very difficult to train, for they are able to go without food for a considerable period, sometimes weeks, with no apparent ill-effects, although I should perhaps state here that none of my eagles have ever been so recalcitrant. But at this stage I was new to the game and I had given in to the whims of my eagle. I only desired to treat him with kindness, not withhold his meals from him. My goal was to attempt to form some sort of bond of affection between us. I made a pair of traditional bewits. These are short strips of leather by which a pair of bells are fitted to the hawk's legs just above the jesses. The bells are a useful ally when searching for a lost hawk because they often betray the presence of the hidden truant when out of sight in a thicket. Many a wayward hawk has been recovered by the faint tinkle of the bells on the wind.

The finest bells were obtained from Lahore in Pakistan, where they were made by an old Pakistani hawk-dealer named Mohammad Din who kept the alloy recipe of the metal a trade secret. It would probably be possible to have the metal analysed in this country and produce them here, but it would scarcely be a lucrative venture for a company to do so on account of the limited demand for hawk bells. Nowadays, serviceable bells are obtainable from dealers in this country who import them from America and elsewhere. These bells, incidently, should be light in weight and one should sound a semi-tone higher than the other. Some falconers prefer to fit a tail bell in addition to, or in place of, the leg bells. The tail bell is fitted on to one of the central tail, or deck feathers, especially in the case of Goshawks or Sparrowhawks, both of whom have the regular habit of shaking their tails on alighting after a flight.

A more modern method of relocating a lost hawk is to fit a bell-sized radio transmitter instead of a bell, thus the movements of the wayward hawk can be tracked with a receiving set which is transistorised and is operated by the falconer himself, rendering it a fairly simple job to home-in on the truant. Although this method is rather expensive it is nevertheless beginning to catch on, especially in America. I added further insult to falconry by fitting almost useless cat bells onto Satan, but it was all there was available at the time.

To reduce feather wear and tear, I abandoned the idea of keeping the birds in cages and made two large outdoor perches out of 8 in plant-pots filled to the brim with concrete and with an 18 in metal spike protruding through the base. This type of perch is known as a block and they are usually made of neatly turned wood or any suitable material that tapers slightly towards the base. The tapering of the block allows the mutes to fall freely to the ground instead of fouling the perch. A fouled perch can be injurious to a hawk's feet, especially if the talons are kept unusually sharp and they happen to puncture the ball of the foot, giving themselves an injection of harmful bacteria, so causing an infection. I fitted two stout metal rings onto the spikes and sank the blocks into the ground to within six inches of the base of the perch. Both blocks were placed near our dense hawthorn hedge which I hoped would act as a wind-break. I was very careful to ensure that neither bird could reach the other on their leashes by spacing them well apart, for I knew that Jappy would stand no chance against Satan. In a very short while I found the block perch method far superior to the cages, the condition of both birds improving immediately.

A friend of mine who was beginning to share my interest in falconry and birds of prey had constructed a lure for me to use when I considered that Satan was ready for that stage in training. This lure consisted of a pair of Black-Headed Gull's wings fastened together with wire in flight posture. Attached to the centre of this contraption was a long tail feather from a cock pheasant, so that when swung around by its length of cord it gave the effect of a bird in flight. This lure, even when modified, was still far too light, so I fitted a heavy wooden handle onto the cord so that it would drag along the ground and slow up any hawk that might try to fly off with it, a not entirely unheard of occurrence with trained raptors.

A winged lure such as this would normally be used with Peregrine or Lanner Falcons, or any other type of long-winged true falcons. The lures used for Goshawks, a short-wing, or eagles and buzzards, which are known as broad-wings, are usually made from stuffed rabbit or hare skins, to which is attached a long line for an assistant to pull or drag along the ground from a distance to simulate a furry running animal. This stuffed lure is generally known as a ground-lure.

When the hawk is flown at prey, or quarry as falconers term it, and she misses her intended victim, as is frequently the case, she may take a stand in some lofty tree or on some electricity pylon and refuse all bribes and oaths to fly back down to the falconer's fist, then the recalcitrant bird may usually be brought down by the movement of the swung lure, in the case of falcons, or the dragging of the ground-lure through grass and nettle beds for Goshawks and eagles. Some hawks become excited at the moving vegetation caused by the dragged lure and yet pay scant attention to their owner's well-garnished fist.

During Satan's first few weeks with me his plumage and outlook changed dramatically. Gone, was the drab, over-sized hawk, in his place was a real eagle with sleek feathers which were now coated with a glossy sheen. The only set-back now was the condition of his feet. They were at times hot to the touch, which indicated infection. There were sore cracks at the joints beneath his toes which I had been filling with ointment, but he had immediately ripped off every sticking plaster that I put on, so that harmful bacteria were free to enter the open wounds. But I had to do something about it because at times he would lie down in pain in the grass beside his block, so one afternoon, with very mixed feelings, I took him indoors and gently but firmly cast him in a dark cloth in such a manner that only his feet and tail were visible. The material was highly porous so that he could easily breathe through it. I had also prepared cotton wool swabs, a scalpel and a pair of forceps which were all soaking in a bowl containing 70 per cent alcohol.

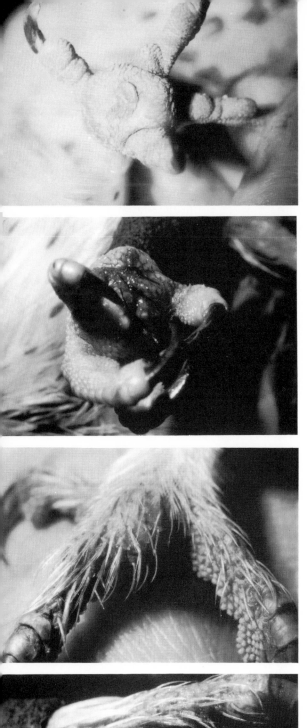

Left *Bumblefoot in a Kestrel. A complaint similar to that affecting Satan.*

Left *Surgical incision to remove Bumblefoot infection.*

Left *Foot of Little Owl, centre digit swollen with infection.*

Left *The infection has been incised but is now neatly stitched*

Block-perch. *Ring-perch.*

I cleaned his feet with a cotton wool swab saturated with alcohol and then, with the scalpel blade, I very carefully cut into one of the worst affected parts. I hadn't a clue as to whether or not I was following the correct procedure, it was the only method I could think of for remedying the malady and I most certainly do not recommend anyone following this procedure without proper veterinary advice. My case was somewhat different in that there were no qualified vets in those days who had any experience with birds of prey and none of the local practitioners relished the job of working on a fully grown eagle.

As soon as the blade had incised the scaly skin, a mixture of blood and pus oozed out, disclosing a firm white, cheese-like core, which was easily removed with the forceps. I then filled up the bleeding cavity with the ubiquitous anti-septic ointment. Even today the aroma given off by this ointment reminds me of those early days. I repeated the operation on two more toes and bandaged them up. He had a couple of smaller sores on other toes, but I considered that he had put up with enough indignities for one day. Within a few days, the treated toes were well on the road to recovery and so I lanced the remaining toes in the same manner. Soon he could grip objects quite normally and he also seemed much happier psychologically, for he would grab pieces of wood that I gave him to play with and pretend that he was killing them. On occasions, he would get carried away with excitement and then stand over his 'kill', panting with his beak wide open for some time afterwards.

I found that my two birds were spending a good deal of their time on the ground and came to the conclusion that the tops of their block perches were too wide and uncomfortable for their feet. They were tree-perching birds really and therefore required ring- or bow-perches, so that they could grip properly. So during one lunch-hour at work, I set about the task of making a pair of bow-perches. Rummaging through a mountain of scrap metal, I came up with two semi-circular pieces of tubular steel which were already a convenient shape. At the apex, where the birds would eventually be perching, I wrapped a thick

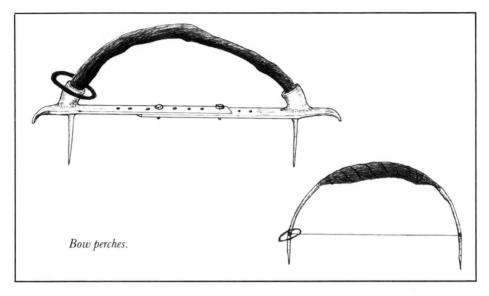

Bow perches.

layer of adhesive fibre tape and tightly bound it with waxed twine. I slid a metal ring along one upright and below this ring, attached a wire trace some 12 in above the ends of each upright. The purpose of this trace was to retain the ring on the perch should the bird happen to pull it out of the ground. With the fitting of the wire trace the completed article closely resembled an old English long-bow, straight from the battlefields of Agincourt or Crécy, hence the name, bow-perch. On arrival home, I sank the perches into the ground up to the wire trace and tethered the leashes of both birds to individual perches. Following the introduction of the bows, both birds spent considerably less time on the ground.

My next acquisition was a good strong plastic referee's whistle, which I blew every time I fed the birds, so instilling into them a sort of Pavlovian reflex. By this I mean that I was getting them accustomed to the sound of the whistle and eventually, I hoped, they would associate this sound with the presentation of their food.

According to the books on falconry that I was now beginning to accumulate, a Goshawk seemed to be the ideal hawk for flying in my type of area and at a wide variety of game. I was also aware that the local dealer was expecting another consignment of Goshawks from Germany and I had already ordered one through him. At this juncture, I began to realise that I was becoming a collector, rather than a falconer. It is practical to keep a minimal number of hawks, because so much time is required with each bird and it is far more desirable to have one bird that is flying properly than several half-trained hawks, therefore, it is false economy to keep a number of birds to fall back on should one happen to be lost. But nevertheless, it is a common fault with many beginners and I was no exception. Fortunately, I had a friend who was interested in falconry and who had taken an interest in Jappy as she was tame and required little looking after. I was very upset to see Jappy go, but I

Above left *Anglo-Indian hood with feather plume.* **Above right** *Arabian hood.* **Below left** *Anglo-Indian hood with a 'Turk's Head' plume.* **Below right** *Falconry Centre pattern hoods.*

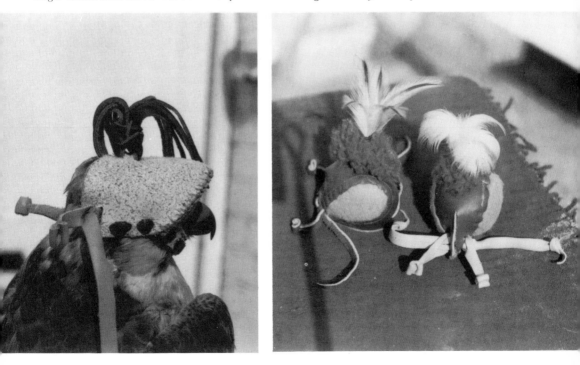

consoled myself with the knowledge that she was going to a good home and would be well cared for, and I could also see her from time to time to follow her progress.

My next necessity was a hood for Satan. Since time immemorial most trained hawks and falcons have had to become accustomed to wearing the hood, which is basically a leather cap that totally blindfolds the bird and renders transportation, imping, coping and rejessing, etc, all the less traumatic. Most hawks will readily tolerate sounds, but very few are not upset by visual disturbances, so the art of hooding becomes a necessary part of the sport. Careful hooding can have a calming effect upon a nervous hawk.

I possessed one hood pattern which was too small for Satan, so I hit on the idea of placing the pattern beneath a friend's photographic enlarger. From this I drew a complete range of patterns by moving the enlarger up and down and drawing around the silhouette projected onto the paper beneath the lamp. Luckily, I already had one or two ready-made hoods and I dismantled one of these piece by piece to discover how they were assembled. The task was very frustrating at first but I soon became deeply involved with the project.

There are several types and variations of hood which include Indian, Arabian, Syrian and Dutch. The hood that I was preparing for Satan was of the Indian pattern with Dutch bracings, a type of hood which I favour above all for, once mastered, they are easy to make and are highly practical. However, they do have to be lightproof and fit properly and I therefore had to keep trying one on Satan and making any necessary modifications. In fact, I had to make three or four hoods before I could obtain one to fit properly. After a short while, with perseverance, he came to accept the strange, plumed, leather cap.

My friend arrived to collect Jappy and shortly afterwards I went to pick up my Goshawk from the dealer. However, unfortunately for me, the order had fallen through and no Goshawks would be arriving for some considerable time. So once more, I found myself glancing at the few remaining birds on the premises, finally selecting an Indian Kestrel.

Chapter 4

Hope and despair

The Kestrel was placed in a cardboard box, whereupon I took it straight home, feeling a mite disappointed. I still longed for a Goshawk, but in the meantime, I would be content to have a go with the Kestrel. The Indian Kestrel is usually a little smaller and a shade lighter than the British version, according to all the individuals that I have seen, although specimens of our own bird can be extremely variable. The Indian sub-species, although often smaller, lacks nothing in courage, as I discovered in later experiences. Once again, I poached a name for her from Reidar Brodtkorb's *Flying Free* and called her 'Eos', after a female Golden Eagle which had gained international acclaim after the Norwegian author had released her to the wild at Loch Katrine in Scotland. My Eos bore no resemblance whatsoever to a Golden Eagle, I merely happened to like the name.

Eos clawed and bit at my hands as I placed a pair of soft calf-skin jesses around her legs. I put on a small swivel of Pakistani origin and a plastic button leash. Such a leash would have been impractical for a stronger bird, such as a Goshawk, but it was ideal for Eos, being rot-proof, strong enough for a Kestrel and did not slip when tied.

For several minutes, Eos bated wildly, but before long she was panting and clinging to my gauntlet. She had already been fed so I could not offer her an immediate mode of friendship. She had plenty of pectoral muscle on her breast and appeared to be in the peak of health. Her eyes were bright and round and her plumage was compact and in excellent condition. I made up my mind there and then that I was going to fly this little bird free.

The following day she was somewhat more approachable and I carried her around the garden, although at one point she nearly fell over backwards when Satan roused himself on his bow-perch by the hedge. I took her to a quiet part of the garden where she would not be disturbed by Satan's preening and set her down upon a rock, keeping a firm hold on the end of her leash. I waggled part of a road-casualty sparrow in front of her and in a flash she jumped from the rock on to my fist and began to tear at the meat for all she was worth. By the time she had finished feeding, her crop was bulging and I was covered with little grey and white feathers from the sparrow.

For the next four days I fed Eos on rabbit meat with no roughage, and after

Above *Eos the Kestrel on a block perch.*

Left *Scales, converted for the weighing of hawks.*

this treatment she lost about 1 oz. After this slight loss of weight, Eos flew readily to the fist as soon as I blew the whistle. The distance she came was only a foot or so, but this was soon increased to four feet, the full length of her leash. Her weight had gradually decreased from $9\frac{1}{2}$ oz to $8\frac{1}{2}$ oz and I discovered that she was much more amiable and attentive at the latter weight. If she was slightly above or below $8\frac{1}{2}$ oz I would run into trouble in my attempts to fly her. If she was overweight, she would simply bob her head and half open her long pointed wings, then close them again and turn her back on me to stare at something of greater attraction in the opposite direction; she just did not want to know. On the other hand, if her weight was too low, she would fly to me all right, but would scream her head off, mantle over her food on my fist and wolf it as if it were the last meal she was likely to see, and then puff out her feathers, refusing to leave the glove. So, needless to say, I kept up the task of weighing her daily and striving to fly her at more or less the same time each day.

The scales I used were of the ordinary kitchen variety, converted for hawk's use by removal of the conventional plastic weighing dish and substituting in its place a wooden perch. Eos automatically took it for some kind of new fangled perch specially put out for her purpose and used it willingly, totally unaware that her weight level was under surveillance.

I had been flying Eos indoors for several days and she would fly across the living room to my outstretched fist for a small piece of meat as soon as I blew the whistle. So I decided that the time had arrived to fly her outside in the garden. Whereas she had been no bother flying to the fist indoors, outside proved to be a very different story. She was more interested in watching the sparrows hopping around the refuse bin, the slightest movement never escaping her attention. Therefore, it was a case of beginning all over again, just as I had done indoors: first a short hop to the fist and then gradually increasing the hop to a flight, and so on. Having no desire to lose her, I kept her on a creance and within a week or so, she was flying the entire length of the garden.

By the middle of the following week she was flying to the fist at a distance of 50 yards on the local playing fields, and it was then that I considered it was time to fly her free, albeit with some trepidation. I had been flying her at 2 pm, but because it was to be her first time free while she had been in my care, I waited until around 3 pm, to ensure that she would be somewhat keener than usual. I carried her to familiar ground where I had been flying her on the creance, or long line, all week and then offered her a tiny scrap of meat from my fingers. She appeared to be as keen as she was ever going to be and so, with an intense feeling of apprehension, I removed her swivel and leash and placed her on a post, free from all encumberances. From a distance of about 20 yards, I gave two sharp blasts on my whistle. She turned to face me, muted, and flew to my fist where she landed like a whisp of thistle-down. She flew again at 50 yards with the same response and I never used the creance on her again. I had trained my first hawk and, provided I kept a tight control on her weight, I could fly her almost anywhere with complete trust.

She was strong on the wing when I took her to Twycross Zoo on the Leicestershire–Warwickshire border one sunny afternoon. I spoke to the zoo's falconer, Mr John Haywood, about the hawks at the zoo for quite some time and, as Eos was keen to fly, John asked me to help him give his public demonstration of falconry. Always glad to oblige, I placed Eos on the mews roof within the zoo grounds and then walked away from her, much further than I had ever done before. I glanced over my shoulder at her, but she was so far distant she was scarcely visible. It was then that I considered I had gone far enough, perhaps too far, so thrusting out my gloved left fist, I emitted two ear-piercing blasts on my whistle that ought to have alerted the Cornish coast-guard. She came immediately and flew like a little gem, hovering for a second or two above my fist before descending on it like an autumn leaf. It was a very proud moment for me, her first flight in public and a good one to boot. Dozens of spectators had watched her in action and were asking all manner of weird and wonderful questions. One lady thought Eos was a thrush with a bent 'nose'.

However, I was painfully aware that this was not true falconry, because the latter is only achieved by flying the bird at living natural quarry. But then, this was only my first serious attempt and it was only a Kestrel; but one day, I vowed, I would fly one of my favourite raptors, the mighty Golden Eagle.

It had occurred to me that I ought to have introduced Eos to a lure long before reaching this stage in her training, but I considered that she was receiving sufficient exercise and was very obedient, so I continued to fist-fly her. Generally speaking, Kestrels are seldom used for serious hawking on account of their small size or, more accurately, the fact that they feed primarily on small rodents and insects renders suitable flights at their natural quarry a rather uninteresting affair. In recent years they have come to the fore as being excellent beginner's birds, but in my opinion, they only fill this category by being relatively easy to obtain at a reasonable price. They have a rather delicate constitution with an indifferent weight factor, and do not suffer negligent and ham-fisted novices gladly. A buzzard is a much more suitable bird for a beginner because of the greater leeway in the weight margin, allowing the would-be falconer more scope for error of judgement, and the possibility that he might just catch something with it at the end of the day.

Satan had tamed considerably since his arrival and I thought it might be to my advantage if I could persuade him to perch on my shoulder as opposed to the fist, as this would render the manning programme more comfortable from the weight point of view. I placed him on my gloved fist and slowly lowered my arm, causing him to side-step up my sleeve and finally on to my shoulder. I practically held my breath in case he should suddenly shoot out one of his heavily armoured feet and catch me full in the face, but he seemed quite content to sit there and remained motionless while I walked around the garden with him. He soon learned what was expected of him and in a surprisingly short time I discovered that he preferred being carried on the shoulder to the fist, and of course, I was able to carry him much further now that I had no aching arm to plague me.

One afternoon, having run short of meat for Satan, I collected him from his grubbing about in the garden, perched him on my shoulder and set off for the

John Haywood with Peregrine Falcon.

butcher's. I had barely reached the end of the grove where we lived when I heard a man hailing me from afar. Approaching, he asked if he could take some photographs of the eagle, never before having observed one at such close quarters. I obliged, whereupon he must have used up an entire film, but it didn't end there. He then produced a cine-camera from his bag and proceeded to put on film the entire trip to the butcher's and back, concluding with the tethering of the bewildered bird to his perch in the back garden. I forgot all about the incident until two days later, when a friend handed me a copy of the *Nottingham Evening Post.* Smack on the front page was a photograph and an accompanying article featuring Satan and me. It was a reasonable write-up and I hoped that any falconers in the area would read it and get in touch with me.

After reading the article it was time to fly Eos, and I ambled down the garden path to take her up from her block. As I approached the block, I thought it odd that she was not greeting me in her usual manner by calling excitedly. I could not see her block from the path as it was screened by dwarf conifers, but she was familiar with the sound of my footsteps and she had never behaved in this manner before. I became quite anxious and my heart missed a beat when I spotted her, huddled on the ground beside her block. It was all that she could manage to utter a feeble piping call. At least, she was still alive and that gave me a chance to get her back to normal again. I assumed that she may have caught a severe cold, but as I picked up her limp form, I noticed that her eyes were glazed and only partly open and she was so thin that her breast-bone resembled the sharp keel of a boat.

I carried her indoors and placed her in a hessian-lined cardboard box in the hearth beside the fire to ensure maximum warmth. I followed up by attempting to force-feed her, for she was far too weak to pull at meat by herself and managed to persuade her to take a few pieces of chopped beef soaked in water to relieve dehydration, but all my efforts were in vain, for by early evening it was all over, she died in my hands and nothing in the world could bring her back. I am not normally the emotional sort, but it took all I could muster to prevent the tears welling up into my eyes. It was while I held her warm, lifeless body close to my chest that I realised how much she had meant to me. They say that you never miss anything until it's no longer there, and it's true. She had been a fine companion and I can but hope she had regarded me in a similar way.

Like all living things, birds of prey are subject to a wide variety of ailments, such as Frounce or Trichomaniasis, a protozoon found in members of the pigeon family which causes whitish plaques in the mouth and throat of hawks, or the killer fungal disease Aspergillosis, caused by the spores of a fungus known to science as *Aspergillus fumigatus* which attacks and destroys the lungs. Many such illnesses often show little or no signs until it is too late. A layman, on studying the body of Eos, could be excused for believing that she had died of starvation, but she always had more than enough food to satisfy her requirements and she was never flown under-weight.

Her death so disturbed me that I parcelled up her body and sent it to Dr John Cooper, a veterinary surgeon studying ailments of raptors at the School of Veterinary Science at Langford, near Bristol. I kept a few of her feathers as a keep-sake, which on reflection was not really the advisable thing to do because a source of infection may have been present in the feathers which could easily, through handling, be transmitted to other birds. It would be at least ten days before I could expect any news from Bristol but when I finally did receive the report from Dr Cooper I was still no wiser as to the cause of her demise. The post-mortem had revealed nothing apart from a slight change in the liver, which apparently was not enough to have killed her. Her death remains one of life's unsolved mysteries. In the meantime I persevered with Satan.

The following day heralded another photograph and article in the *Daily Express*, this time with a different photograph. But it still did little to ease my sunken spirits caused by the sudden death of Eos. The only method that I could think of to help take my mind off her was to begin a serious training programme on Satan.

I brought him indoors and placed him on an upturned box, then, armed with a juicy lump of beef, I held out my gloved fist about a foot away from him, trying to tempt him to come for it by waggling the meat about enticingly in front of his beak. He eyed me suspiciously and could not fathom out what the devil I was playing at. He then tried to snatch the meat, first with one foot and then the other. Finally, after craning his neck to its fullest extent, he half-opened his wings and jumped onto my fist. I repeated the exercise and after much whistle-blowing on my part, he came once more. I allowed him a small crop of food after his second death-defying leap and then returned him to his bow-perch to digest it. He was well over flying weight, which meant that the next few weeks would have to be spent on getting him into hunting condition.

The next evening, I hurried home from work to give Satan his next lesson. I sorted out a few choice cuts and went outside to offer them to him. Seconds later, I was shocked and horrified. His bow-perch was empty. All that remained was a few inches of leather leash attached to the metal ring on the perch. I suspected a fault in the leather, because it had been a strong, brand new leash and he could not possibly have snapped it in so short a time had the leather not been faulty. First Eos, and now Satan. Two birds gone in one week and Satan was off on his own with a good head start.

Chapter 5

The search for Satan

Over the past few weeks, Satan and Eos had become a large part of my every-day existence. Most of my life revolved around them. I seldom went far without one or the other of them and they were infinitely more valuable to me than anything else I had ever possessed. Now both were gone. Eos's death had been so final, but somewhere in the neighbourhood, Satan was still at large. While I knew he was still alive, I would be most reluctant to give up any hunt for him.

My father had been at home all afternoon but had been engrossed in tidying up the front garden. He had seen Satan about one hour previously and the eagle was still sitting quietly on his perch then, so I considered that there was a reasonable chance that he was still in the immediate vicinity. There was a farm beyond our back garden wall and because this was the most open piece of land in the area, I took it for granted that he may have taken that route. I ran along the road to the far side of the farm and splashed across the dyke which bordered the farmland, separating it from all the surrounding property. As I was struggling up a bank of loose soil on the farm side of the dyke, a man called to me from one of a row of nearby houses. He said that my eagle was perched in one of two Lombardy poplar trees which were growing about 30 yards from the dyke and about 100 yards from our back wall.

My father and brother arrived on the scene on the opposite side of a tall wire-netting fence which ran between the two towering trees. They too had seen Satan fly up into the poplar from the field just beyond our garden wall. I could not see him from the ground and because the trees were virtually unclimbable, I lobbed several pieces of turf into the branches until he came out; when he did, the sight was absolutely breathtaking. He soared and spiralled on his six foot spread of wing, looking for all the world like a barn-door flying about. The sky was a vivid blue, the sun catching for a brief instant the tawny colour of his body. I felt a surge of pride that I was the owner of that magnificent spectacle. Even if I never recaptured him, it seemed almost worthwhile to watch him wheeling about the azure sky on his broad sails. He circled above our garden for some time and at one point even attempted to land on his abandoned perch, but the wind proved too strong for him and he was lifted skywards again like a giant kite, where he soared away to land on a neighbour's roof. He ran along the top of the roof and jumped on to the chimney stack where he rested for several minutes, only to rise again and come to rest on a bungalow two avenues away, surprising a ginger tomcat who had chosen that particular spot to sunbathe. Fortunately for the cat, Satan took off again almost immediately, this time towards the local cemetery. He was beginning to make a considerable height gain when dozens of gulls, which had been feeding nearby, rose into the air and began to dive-bomb him, forcing him down to grass-top level. Then came the opportunity that I had been waiting for. Satan had run out of high perching places, temporarily, and for the first time since his escape he came to rest on the ground in the cemetery between two gravestones.

Half-climbing and half-falling over the railings that enclosed the cemetery, I raced towards him in a frantic bid to close the gap between us. I was almost upon him when he spread his great wings and allowed the wind to carry him across the graveyard. I was beginning to succumb to exhaustion by this time and being no great long-distance runner and, in addition, a slight asthma sufferer, I shortly became lacking in breath and was wheezing and croaking like a frog. But even so, I was determined to try and catch him by nightfall, for he still had a swivel and a foot or so of leash attached to his jesses. The main cause of my anxiety here was the fact that the swivel forms the jesses into a 'V' shape, which can easily become snarled up on a variety of projections, such as tree branches. I pictured Satan hanging upside down for days on end to die the miserably slow death of starvation. With this predicament deeply etched on my mind I spurred on my attempts and followed the route in which I had last seen him flying.

When I eventually located him I thought for a few brief moments that I had him trapped, for he had flown from the cemetery and had come to rest between two large buildings that formed part of a small factory. His only ways of absconding further were to either fly up vertically, a very difficult task for an eagle of his proportions, or fly between the deadly wires of a high barbed-wire fence. He accomplished the latter with consummate skill. Not one feather touched any part of that fence, which I believed to be quite a feat for such a young and 'inexperienced' bird like Satan. It was obvious that I had well and truly underestimated his capabilities and he had now rammed home this oversight in no uncertain terms. It was plainly obvious that I was going to have my work cut out for me in my efforts to recapture him. The numerous walls, railings, hedges, fences and gardens that Satan took easily in his stride, were becoming an ever increasing hazard for me as I was becoming more and more weary by the minute and each new fence seemed ten feet higher than the last. Everything seemed somehow unreal and, in addition, I was seething with frustration as I shakily scrambled over awkward obstacles, eventually spearing myself in the stomach while climbing over a set of spiked metal railings. After this mishap, I had no other choice than to halt for a rest, for I could scarcely breathe. Satan had become temporarily lost and my father, brother and a few friends who had joined in the hunt were nowhere to be seen. I slowly made my way back to the nearest main road where I was joined by my brother, and shortly afterwards, by my father. My friends had long since given up finding

Satan came to rest in the cemetery.

that the hard going had knocked most of the fun and excitement out of it all.

As for Satan, we knew that he was perched somewhere in one of the many surrounding trees, but the problem was that the majority of these were in private gardens and it isn't done to go bounding all over the residents' petunias. We plodded on further down the road and obtained permission to continue the search on a large plant nursery which had been in the path of Satan's last visible line of flight, and I spent the next half hour or so wading through neck high in a nettle bed and struggling through a tangled mass of brambles, whose spines insisted upon hooking themselves into my flesh and whose trailing stems wrapped around my legs in attempts to pull me onto their bayonet-like appendages. If he was anywhere in this jungle of weeds, he was certainly making full use of the cover.

It had also occurred to me that he might not be in this particular area at all and that people elsewhere could be sending in valid reports of his whereabouts to my home. It seemed futile to continue scouring the nursery, so I temporarily gave up the search and returned home. My brother remained at home to answer any such calls while I went to inform the local newspaper of the escape and also to assure the local population that the eagle would not pose a threat to their children.

After giving all the relevant details to the newspaper, I returned home, where my mother informed me that a man had been in a car and driven my brother to the spot where Satan was alleged to be perching. Apparently, he was sitting on a house roof in Redland Grove, to the rear of the local health clinic. I left home immediately and ran hard all the way, fighting off an attack of 'stitch' which had begun to plague me. I presently arrived at Redland Grove to find my brother, and several other people, gazing up at the tawny form, still perched on the house roof and defying all attempts at recapture. There was little I could do while he remained on this lofty perch. He certainly would not come to me for food as his training programme was not that far advanced and he was well over flying weight in any case. Had I tried to climb up to him he would no doubt have taken to the air and in this area, with its super-abundance of houses and trees, he would have been very difficult to relocate.

My brother informed me that Satan had come out from beneath a hawthorn bush in the plant nursery just across the way, the same nursery in which I had previously spent a somewhat painful half-hour. In the meantime however, Satan decided that the roof-top was not such an ideal place on which to spend the night, so he made the next move. With one wide sweep of his great wings he abandoned his lofty perch and sailed over the roof-tops towards the clinic and became lost from view once more. My brother and I made our way to Burton Road in front of the clinic, where we mutually agreed that the grounds surrounding the latter would be as good a place as any to resume the search, so, without losing any more valuable time, owing to the rapid advance of nightfall, we tried to make good our intentions. The search of the grounds proved fruitless, having failed to catch even a glimpse of the elusive bird.

There was a fairly large stretch of open ground beyond the clinic that held several large trees and so we decided to concentrate our efforts on that area. The rapidly sinking sun had painted the sky with multi-coloured shades of red, tinged here and there with patches of yellow, blue and purple, silhouetting everything that stood against this panoramic setting. Soon everywhere would be shrouded in the dark blanket of nightfall, and my only hope now was to try and find him again before total sunset, and if possible, climb up to his chosen roost after dark. But we still had to find him and it was becoming darker and darker by the minute.

Before long, both my brother and I became aware of a large gathering of noisy blackbirds coming from one of the trees in the clinic grounds. From past experience with wild birds of prey, such a gathering generally heralds the presence of a predatory bird or animal. The song-birds vary their alarm calls according to whether the intruder is a hawk or a four-footed predator, such as a cat, or a fox. These blackbirds seemed to have pin-pointed an avian predator, even though it might only be a roosting Kestrel or a Tawny Owl setting out on his nocturnal jaunt. Either way, I did not have a great deal of time to waste speculating, so we rapidly retraced our steps back to the clinic.

Most of the song-birds flew off at our approach, but a handful of them remained long enough to give us a bearing on their cause for concern. It was Satan right enough. He was glaring down at us from the leafy bough of a tree. I placed a large, tempting piece of beef on the ground beneath his tree and secured it with a wooden stake, in the faint hope that he might come down to it and give me another chance at him. But he was not to be had and remained perched aloft. I certainly named him aptly when I called him Satan. The strange part about it is that both my brother and I had checked this very tree sometime earlier and had over-looked him. All that we could do now was to wait until nightfall.

My brother went home to inform my parents of my whereabouts and what I was planning to do. As the evening drew to a close it grew bitterly cold, and I was only wearing a pair of faded jeans and a thin nylon shirt. I spent a very chilly hour in the clinic doorway sitting on my gauntlet on the cold stone steps. After all the previous excitement and running about, this last hour seemed the longest and hardest part of all, a sort of anti-climax. However, my father joined me some time later to bring me a warm jacket and from then on, with having someone to talk to, the time seemed to pass much faster. We could observe Satan from where we were sitting and could record any of his movements, although it soon became apparent that he was quite prepared to spend the night there, and so, about one hour after the last light faded, I made my move.

There was a fairly strong wind blowing and this, together with the bright orange sodium light from a street lamp shining into his eyes, would, I hoped, prevent him from spotting me too soon. In fact, for the first time since his escape, everything seemed to point in my favour. Even the noise from the passing traffic in the road below would help to make my ascent all the more easier. I had to shin up the first part of the tree as there were no convenient low branches and, to make matters more distasteful, the trunk was coated with a thick layer of soot-like dust which had been sprayed up from the road for decades. This dust came away from the bark in great clouds and found its way into my eyes and mouth. However, I gradually made my way up to the first branches; Satan still being some 25 feet above me, it was a nightmare of a climb up the remainder of the tree. The road far below was busy with heavy traffic and it was quite an unnerving experience to have great heaving juggernauts trundling at speed directly below.

I estimated that I still had about another ten feet or so to climb when I became aware of a large shadowy figure perched on a branch level with my head. It was Satan, and he was close enough to observe that his jesses and leash, which I was hoping to grab, were beneath his feet, literally, he was standing on them. This would no doubt have come about when he threw his feet forward to land in the tree, the same action also throwing the jesses forwards so that he would land on them. I had often seen him do this on his bow-perch and he would sit there looking most uncomfortable. It certainly reduced my chances of catching him quite considerably. The only other alternative was to try and reach for one of his legs, which I almost accomplished with one energetic leap, but I was only successful in grabbing one of his tail feathers as he swept out of the tree towards the cemetery. In desperation I almost flew out after him. It was now apparent that he was not going to get himself caught this night for it was too dark to organise another search. Utterly disappointed and dejected, I scrambled back down the tree to rejoin my father who was patiently waiting below.

On the way back home I made a brief inspection of the cemetery, but to no avail. I had already made up my mind that I would have to take the next day off from work to continue the search before he went too far afield. My eyes scanned the macabre spectacle of the cemetery, which was rendered infinitely more eerie by an inky black sky studded with a million glittering stars and a slight ground mist. The stark, shadowy silhouettes of a group of Scots pine trees were just visible above the white marble gravestones, and yet, somewhere in this ghoulish landscape, somewhere out there, was Satan, a bird whom, in the past few months had come to mean something special to me.

I went home to bed but my head was so full of thoughts that I could not sleep a wink, and the various wounds that I had sustained during the evening were now beginning to ache and throb and make their presence felt. It has never ceased to amaze me how one can sustain fearful injuries during a course of excitement or danger and yet feel no pain until the excitement subsides. I was now nursing a number of hitherto unknown cuts and abrasions. I lay awake for most of the night and even when I did manage to doze off for a few brief moments, I was rudely awakened in sharp starts and then began to drift into dreams, wondering what events, if any, the morrow would bring. Would I ever find him again? I repeatedly had visions of myself catching him in various ways and situations, and thinking how different things might have been had his jesses been hanging down in the normal fashion.

In the morning I made a daylight search in the cemetery, questioning several council workmen in the grounds, but they merely shook with mirth, suggesting that I might try the Highlands of Scotland. However, I did manage to extract some information from one of the lads who worked in the cemetery greenhouses. He told me that Satan had landed behind the range of greenhouses shortly after midnight and had spent the entire night there. If only I had received that information some ten hours earlier. Typical of Satan, he was now not to be found anywhere in or around the cemetery, so I decided that the best policy would be to return home and await news of his whereabouts coming in.

I did not have long to wait. At around 11 am, two officers from the City Police drew up in a patrol car and informed me that the truant Satan was perched on a lamp-post near Manor Road, very close to where I had put him out of the tree the previous evening. I picked up my rifle and proceeded to the spot as fast as I could. If I failed to capture Satan this day, I had regretfully resolved to shoot him personally and spare him the agonies of getting his jesses caught up in the branches of some tree and there hang head downwards, until exhaustion and starvation claimed him, a fact which rendered me miserable with guilt and shame over my incapacity or neglect at checking his equipment.

As I ran along Burton Road towards the clinic, I saw a group of 20 or 30 people gazing up at the bewildered bird as he perched on the top of the lamp-post, which was by some incredible coincidence, the same lamp-post that had provided me with the light to ascend his tree the previous night. It seemed strange that he should have found his way back there again. He obviously recognised me amongst all those people, because he saw me arrive and immediately launched himself into the air. I personally believe that most trained hawks can pick out their own handlers in a crowd as several later experiences have proved. In fact, many raptorial birds often express a certain affection towards their owners to the exclusion of all others.

Satan was making full use of all the trees in the area but the blackbirds and sparrows soon revealed his whereabouts. Eventually, he came to rest in a garden on Manor Road; I shall never forget the expression on the face of the occupant of the house when I informed her that my eagle was perched upon her garden fence. She couldn't see the bird from the back door of her house so we ventured down the garden path with the result that Satan left his concealed perch and swooped low down over her herbaceous borders and rose bed, cleared the opposite fence and departed once more. I hastily thanked the lady for her co-operation and left her standing in the garden, mouth agape and quite speechless. Evidently, news of his escape had not previously reached her ears.

Satan flew off across the main road and then was lost to sight. All I could do now was to wander aimlessly in the direction that he had taken, which I did and finally ended up on nearby Conway Road, where an elderly gentleman told me that he had seen the eagle from his front garden, flying through a gap between two houses in an adjoining road. One of the owners of the houses kindly allowed me to pass through his property and even pointed Satan out to me. The scoundrel was perched on top of a railway embankment which bordered the rear gardens of the houses. I crept along a grass verge at the base of the embankment and then, the very instant that he spotted me, I rushed him. He bungled his take-off in his haste to get away and I almost managed to grab his trailing leash, but the wind was in his favour and he flew down the railway track at a rate of something like 60 or 70 miles an hour. He soared out over an adjoining cricket field, then altered direction and flew back across the railway lines and settled amongst a large group of hawthorn bushes. About a dozen or so rooks gathered above him and commenced their mobbing tactics, cawing loudly. He took off yet again, spiralling higher and higher and then allowed the air currents to carry him towards Gedling Woods, which were situated about one mile to the north. I attempted to follow him on foot but soon became hampered by bramble covered slopes and large stretches of open water, so I gave up and went home, fully realising that it would take nothing short of a miracle to catch him now.

The following evening I received two reports, one from the borough of Arnold and the other from the churchyard at Burton Joyce. He seemed to be having such an affinity with churches and graveyards, I began to wonder if his name had anything to do with it. The latter report was by far the most logical because Arnold was situated in the opposite direction and upwind from the route that Satan was known to be taking. Something was definitely stirring in Arnold, and, as the report came from a relation of my friend Chris Mills and as we could also get a lift by car, we decided to check it out. But as usual, 'the bird had flown' by the time we arrived there. I found out some time later that the bird had been an escaped Black Kite *(Milvus migrans)*, but I never did find out who lost it.

Luckily, the day after was a Saturday, and the morning found my father and

I at the churchyard in the village of Burton Joyce. One village resident told us that Satan had moved into the adjoining village of Bulcote. We thoroughly searched the area and ended up on the sewage farms at Bulcote. As youngsters, we used to call this part of the countryside 'Gull Island', on account of the multitudes of gulls that annually nested there. We spent quite some time watching Ringed Plovers and Great Crested Grebes, my father finding that his Praktica Super TL camera, fitted with a 300 mm telephoto lens was very useful for birdwatching.

I received no more reports until the following Tuesday, when the Carlton Police telephoned me at work with the news that Satan was perched on yet another lamp-post; he seemed to have an affinity with lamp-posts as well as graveyards, only this time it was in the village of Rolleston, near Newark. He was moving far afield now and was a good 20 miles from home. Obtaining permission to leave work, I went home to collect my rifle and gauntlet and caught the next train to Newark.

My biggest problem was where to start. The surrounding open farmland covered a vast area and really needed a fully organised search party. In desperation, I chose a picturesque country lane leading off on my left towards Rolleston, and before long came upon two farm-lads to whom I promptly furnished details of my quest. They had seen Satan the previous evening down the river at Fiskerton, with a 'chain' on his legs. I had already passed through this village on my way to Rolleston, but I continued on my way for the police message did state that Satan was perched on a lamp-post in Rolleston Village.

There appeared to be only two lamp-posts in the entire village, one at either end and a short trip to each of them rendered it obvious that he had moved elsewhere. Three highly amused farm-hands told me they had seen no eagles but they had seen a huge bull African elephant charging around the wheatfields only that morning. Not being in the mood for any such jokes, and resisting the temptation to 'give them a barrel', I departed from their midst and continued down the lane until it petered out into a field of recently-sown barley. I espied a large pale brown shape huddled in the centre of the field. Surely, I thought, it couldn't be Satan. However, with hopes raised once more, I pelted over the soft brown earth at a fantastic rate of knots, only to come face to face with the expressionless dial of an old buck hare, which promptly leapt from its form and gave me a lesson in running. I had had enough for one day and resolved that I would not go out after Satan again unless I received a more recent report. On the way back to the country lane two women hailed me from their front gardens. They had realised I was looking for the eagle and indeed it was one of them who had originally sent the message of Satan's whereabouts. She also told me that the last time she saw Satan, he had been flying towards the plantation.

The plantation turned out to be an area of densely planted pine trees, not unlike parts of Thieves' Wood, a plot of land where he could most easily snarl up his jesses. There had been intermittent showers all day, but now the sky was rapidly growing darker, and lightning was beginning to flash above the skyline. Then came the deluge, wave upon wave of driving rain, coupled with roars of thunder. Regrettably, I had to abandon the search and dismally caught the next train back to Nottingham. As I watched the beads of rainwater carving paths down the windows of the carriage, I allowed my thoughts to wander again. Had it not rained so severely, and had I properly searched the plantation, it is just conceivable that I might have found him.

The newspapers were still publishing articles concerning Satan's escape, but whole weeks were passing without a single report of his movements coming in. It seemed certain that he had finally hung himself up somewhere, possibly among the trees in the plantation at Rolleston. I had a longing for another eagle and would not be fully satisfied until I had another one sat in the garden. The majority of falconers generally dislike the use of eagles on account of their uncertain dispositions and great bulk, which can make them unwieldy in the field and, even when trained, some eagles will turn on their owners on occasion, sometimes leaving great ugly gouges on some part of their unprotected person. But in my opinion, I believe that most falconers regard eagles as cumbersome giants because they have only seen them flown in flat English meadows and the like, whereas in reality they are no more designed for this type of flight any more than a Peregrine Falcon is built to fly and hunt in dense pine forests.

If one casts off a really fit, well-trained eagle in mountainous or hilly terrain one will see a bird in its element, styled to perfection, where it can soar on out-stretched wings hundreds of feet above the earth. I have since watched sights like this many times, and the death-dealing stoop at a rabbit from such a height is certainly equal to anything that I have seen performed by the princely Peregrine. Unfortunately, however, few falconers have the opportunity, or the inclination, to watch such a spectacle, preferring to hunt with the larger falcons or the Goshawk.

Some time after the loss of Satan, it came to my notice that a bird farm in Derbyshire had advertised a number of birds of prey for sale, so the first free morning that came my way, I visited the farm with my Uncle 'bionic' Alan who had been spending a few days with us. As we neared our destination, we came upon an attractive country lane illuminated with purple knapweed flowers. Both Five- and Six-Spotted Burnet Moths swayed in a drunken stupour to and fro over the flowers like gaudy scarlet and green bees.' Their discarded silken cocoons could still be seen adhering to the grass stems in large numbers. Here and there, large shrubs of honeysuckle draped themselves over the dry stone walls which are so much a feature of the Derbyshire countryside. The scent from the bizarre flowers of the honeysuckle was almost intoxicating as it wafted its way gently down the lane on a warm, gentle breeze.

The bird farm was situated at the end of this lane and consisted of a great array of wire-mesh aviaries surrounding an old white-washed farmhouse and outbuildings. The proprietor had advertised some Eagle Owls but these had since been sold. He had a pair of Saker Falcons *(Falco cherrug)* and a Brahminy Kite *(Haliastur indus)* in an indoor aviary, but at this stage of my falconry career, I had not as yet taken a great deal of interest in falcons and the Kite did not really appeal to me. We were on the verge of leaving the premises, for we thought that this was the sum total of raptorial birds in stock, when the dealer suggested that we have a look in the flights to the rear of the house. These contained a great variety of birds ranging from Blue Magpies and Reeve's Pheasants to what I originally took to be a pair of Golden Eagles. I nearly fell through the floor with amazement when I caught sight of them. The male was not a great deal larger than Satan and was deep in the moult, but the female was one of the largest eagles that I had ever set eyes upon. She was also moulting but was in much better condition than the male. Finding these two like this was like the answer to a prayer. I possessed an insatiable desire to own the female, but the dealer required the king's ransom of £65 for her.

The eagle looked so powerful and magnificent as she flew across the flight that I knew I just had to make the decision and bought the bird. At long last, I thought to myself, a Golden Eagle of my very own.

Chapter 6

Aquila and the BBC

After constructing a rough wooden box from some old timbers, the dealer and I entered the aviary to catch the winged monster. She flew from her perch and clung for all she was worth to the wire mesh. Her feet were so powerful that they bent and contorted the wire into incredible shapes. She was loaded with fight, but eventually released her grip on the wire and threw herself on to her back where she presented us with both sets of formidable talons, which she thrust at us with alarming ferocity and buffeted us with her gigantic wings, sending the pair of us sprawling. We eventually managed to grab her legs and after carefully folding her wings in the natural position alongside her body, she was transferred thus to the awaiting box.

I was none too keen on putting her in the rough-sided box for she could easily injure herself were she to struggle, but it seemed the only suitable way of getting her home. We draped the box with a length of hessian and bound the latter securely with string, out of which we also fashioned two carrying handles. The box was bouncing all over the place as the great bird thrashed at the wood-work, and the journey home seemed endless. We were still on the first of two buses when it appeared that the box would not withstand much more of her battering and I fully expected her to break out and assault the passengers at any moment. Fortunately, more by luck than design, we arrived home with the box intact, which we placed on the floor of the conservatory while I informed my father of our lucky find.

Returning to the conservatory, I removed the hessian and forced off two or three strips of wood that had formed part of the lid and then retired to fetch my gauntlet. By the time I returned, the eagle had smashed her way out of the box and was perched on top of it. She was a picture of absolute ferocity and was in a really ugly mood after her recent course of indignities. She elevated her crown of hackles at me and I began to wonder how on earth I was going to be able to put a pair of jesses on her. I had already made a pair of jesses while informing my father of my acquisition, but I had had to make a wild guess at the circumference of her legs.

The actual fitting of the jesses turned out to be a far more manageable exercise than I had anticipated. After the initial restraining, she lay with her back on my legs as I sat in an armchair and she did not even attempt to strike me. Her behaviour was now fields apart from that she had exhibited in the aviary. Within minutes, she was walking about the house, gazing at the supple leather about her feet. On account of her great size and strength, and also because leather had previously let me down with Satan, I used a 5 ft long button leash made of braided nylon with a breaking strain of several thousand pounds. The Hardy's deep sea swivel that I used had a breaking strain of 150 lb, so I was reasonably confident that any chances of escape from the faulty equipment point of view were remote. I spent the remainder of the afternoon trying to persuade the eagle to perch on my fist, but all was in vain. The very best that she accomplished was to lay across my gauntlet like a great fat hen, which, combined with her weight, was a very trying experience for me.

Next morning, the eagle was in a much more tractable mood and I was able to offer her a few tit-bits which she took greedily from my fingers. I tried manning her all morning, but she only perched on my gauntlet for a few fleeting moments before bating off again. She bit through my frail gauntlet with ease and frequently used this as a pastime if nothing else attracted her attention. She continuously savaged one particular part of the glove until my blood began to seep through the leather, causing me excruciating pain as she twisted and tore at my knuckles. I also very nearly lost an eye on account of this huge and savage beak and I actually did lose several chunks of flesh from my face, but I refused to admit defeat and was 100 per cent determined not to let her get the better of me. Time and patience would win in the end I assured

Aquila raised her hackles at me.

Aquila finally consented to perch upon my fist.

myself, but we were in no mood for each other's company that day and I thought it prudent to allow her to spend the next day sitting quietly on her perch to give her more time to contemplate and take stock of the situation.

Once again, my family sat about the house trying to think up a suitable name for my latest acquisition and eventually, my father came up with 'Aquila', after the eagles' generic name. Aquila was destined to become quite a milestone in my future falconry activities, for she was the toughest, most stubborn and recalcitrant predatory bird that it has been my fortune, or misfortune, to handle.

On her third day of training, Aquila finally consented to perch in the accepted manner upon my fist. I had previously considered Satan a 'hard-case', but he had taken a mere four and a half hours to get the message. After this great triumph I attempted walking down the road with her upon my fist, but to my disappointment, although it was only to be expected, she bated at the passing of every car and she clouted me heavily on the back of my head with her great wings on numerous occasions. She still continuously slashed and hacked at my hands with her powerful beak, ripping my knuckles to shreds. It appeared to me that she herself had decided that enough forward moves had been made for one day and didn't want to play anymore, so I again deemed it prudent to return her to the perch.

She was certainly well overweight and I knew that before she would co-operate willingly with my demands, there would need to be a certain amount of reduction of this excess of flesh. To achieve this desirable state of affairs, I reduced her daily ration of food slightly and kept a record of her weight loss, or gain, in a book after weighing the bird daily before feeding. Even after the loss of over 1 lb, she still seemed as intractable as ever, so in desperation, I tried her on a course of washed meat, which has long been a method used by falconers in the past. I bought a quantity of fresh lean beef and soaked it in a bowl of water which I kept in the refrigerator for 24 hours or so, changing the bloody water at frequent intervals. At the end of that period, I squeezed the strips of beef in a clean cloth to ring out the last of the nutrients. The idea behind this method is that although the bird receives its full quota of food by volume, thereby keeping the digestive system in full working order, the washed beef, lacking in blood and presumably vitamins too, causes a reduction in weight through lack of sufficient nourishment. Suffice it to say, that courses of washed meat should be short in duration, limited to a few days at a time and the bird should not be called to the fist for such unpalatable food. So for the next few days, I placed her ration of 6 oz of washed meat on a slab of stone beside her perch. I scalded this stone daily with a kettle full of boiling water to reduce any chances of infection from shreds of decaying meat that might otherwise have adhered and collected harmful bacteria. It is a well-known fact that most eagles will consume all manner of decaying carrion, but I could see little point in inviting sources of infection.

Even after the washed meat course was completed, Aquila still panicked and bated away at my approach. I tried manning her up and down the road again and this time met with greater success. She bated perhaps half a dozen times as I walked down the road, but only bated once as I walked back up again. She was learning gradually, but I considered that she was still slightly overweight, so after three days of normal feeding on 4 oz of meat, I put her on another course of three days of washed meat.

She was a much heavier bird than Satan and my arm ached considerably if I carried her for prolonged periods without a rest. Her wing-span was almost eight feet and she measured three feet from the extremity of her beak to the tip of her tail. Her beak, an implement with which she was extremely handy, was greyish and of immense proportions while her feet were likewise, although these were whitish in colour, not the usual vivid yellow. Unlike Satan, I was relieved to observe, she suffered no talon or foot damage. She was half-way through the moult and her new plumage was a much darker shade of brown. She had the typical white carpal patches on the wings of the immature Golden Eagle, but her tail was entirely dark brown, not white with a dark brown terminal band as it ought to have been.

After this second course of washed meat, the manning programme with Aquila seemed to improve rapidly. She soon overcame her innate fear of traffic, but she objected most strongly whenever I attempted to use both hands to bear her weight. Unfortunately, she never lost this rather annoying habit and whenever I tried to ease the strain of carriage, I was instantly rewarded

Above *The fierce stare of Aquila, the Pallas's Sea Eagle.*

Below *Aquila slashed at me with her powerful beak.*

with a quick slash from her cutlass of a beak and a dose of her furious bating.

Before long, Aquila and I appeared in the *Nottingham Evening Post*, with Aquila being noted as Satan's successor. The same evening that we appeared in the paper, I received a card from the local newspaper office requesting that I telephone the latter that same evening. Apparently, a representative had called with the card and informed my mother that it was something to do with television. Having nothing better to do that evening, I telephoned the news-paper and was duly informed that the BBC wished to film Aquila and I for a television programme the following evening. As Aquila was in fine condition I agreed to do it. I was engrossed in making a spare pair of jesses when the camera team arrived. Three large cars drew up outside our house and out of each one came several technicians and cameramen, each carrying a fantastic array of photographic and recording paraphernalia. While the cameras were being positioned, I prepared some strips of beef as they required some film sequences of Aquila feeding on my fist. I anticipated that beef would be the best food to use, for the sight of an eagle ripping up something like a day-old chick would, I thought, probably upset someone.

Meanwhile, Aquila, who had been quietly observing all the proceedings with growing interest, eagerly stepped onto my gauntlet when the time came to take her up. She raised her hackles in defiance as a large zoom-lens focused on her head and she threatened the cameraman behind it. Finding that she could not

Aquila posed for the BBC film crew.

Aquila threatened the BBC cameraman.

reach him, she slashed at me instead, taking a piece out of my eyebrow. However, still smiling and attempting to staunch the flow of blood discreetly, I began to speak into the microphone. This was my first experience with television and I was petrified, stammering over my words and allowing my mind to go blank for seconds at a time, but eventually, and with the kind understanding of the presenter, I was able to concentrate fully on the questions put to me, which I answered far more efficiently than I had dared hope.

The shots of Aquila feeding on the fist were obtained and for the final part I had to take her out for a walk in the grove, the cameras still being trained on us. Luckily, the cameras were on the wrong side to record Aquila taking a second chunk out of the same eyebrow, but still managing to raise a smile, I proceeded to walk down the grove. I could not help thinking that had they tried to film this part a few weeks previously, the result would have been entirely different. Aquila performed well and the crew obtained some fine shots of her as she spread her wings against the oncoming wind. The whole filming process seemed to last an eternity and I was filled with anxiety over the thought that I might make some stupid blunder. Three reels of film were used up and after the last of the camera crew piled into their car and drove away, I gave Aquila the remainder of her interrupted meal and set her down on her perch for the night. The film was due to be sent to the studios the following Monday, but for some unknown reason I had my doubts as to whether it would be used. Somehow, I could not visualise myself on television. However, it had not all been in vain, for on the following Tuesday evening, about five minutes of the film was shown on BBC television on a programme called 'Midlands Today', introduced by Tom Coyne.

*   *   *

One weekend, I paid the Wilford dealer another visit and espied on a screen-perch in one of the sheds, an eyas Great Horned Owl *(Bubo virginianus)*. I took an instant liking to this bird and spent the best part of half an hour simply gazing at it. I judged by its relatively small size that it was probably a male, but although I say smallish, it was still three times the size of the largest Tawny Owl. Its head was covered with juvenile 'down' feathers and only one 'ear tuft' had protruded as yet. Its eyes were remarkably striking, the pupils being jet-black while the irises were a beautiful shade of canary yellow, each being almost as large as a 50p piece. Its white breast was heavily barred with black while the remainder of the body, including the wings, was buffish, finely peppered and barred with dark bown. During my study of the bird I was threatened by much hissing and beak snapping and it flashed its white throat locket at me.

I desired the bird as it was at the right age for taming—adults rarely tame satisfactorily—so I left the dealer's premises with the thought of raising £25, the dealer's asking price for the owl, ringing in my head. It must be very satisfying to be so well-off financially that one can afford to buy one's desires outright; for every offer that came my way I had to keep on making sacrifices, my weekly earnings being meagre. The only consolation with my method was

Screen-perch; type of perch used by the Wilford dealer.

Above *Archimedes, or Archie,*
as a youngster before he developed
his full ear-tufts.

Left *Archie flashed his white*
throat locket at me.

that at least it made one appreciate one's hard won possessions.

The following day I received a most unexpected and welcome letter from a Mr Sam Barnes of Pwllheli, North Wales. It turned out that the BBC had written to Mr Barnes and informed him that I owned a Mongolian Golden Eagle and he was asking for such particulars as Aquila's weight and colouration. Mr Barnes owned a sub-species of Golden Eagle known in the Kirghiz and Russian steppes of Khazakstahn as the Berkute, or Berkut. His bird was a female named Atalanta and he kindly enclosed a newspaper cutting of himself, Atalanta and Shep, his enormous sheepdog who had been trained to find the eagle in all the inaccessible nooks and crannies of the local mountain ranges and then worry her until she flew home.

Atalanta came from the Himalayas and was trained out there to protect the herds of livestock from wolf depredations. Mr Barnes bought her from a tribesman on a zoological expedition. In my reply to his letter, I sent the information Mr Barnes required plus several photographs and slides. I also explained that, to the best of my knowledge, Aquila was not Mongolian and I could not comprehend how the BBC had drawn that conclusion. Mr Barnes's rapid reply to my letter was full of useful information on the keeping of Golden Eagles. He had studied my photographs, which unfortunately were not quite so pristine as they might have been, but he seemed reasonably certain that Aquila was a Golden Eagle.

Later in the week I revisited the premises of the Wilford dealer and found that, much to my delight, the Great Horned Owl still remained unsold. During my stay at Wilford, I met Brian Ford at that time drummer for Billy Fury's backing group, *The Plainsmen*, who was very keen on falconry. Brian drove me back home as he wished to see Aquila. He was mainly interested in Goshawks, but nevertheless we struck up what was to be a life-long friendship.

In the meantime, I could not forget the Great Horned Owl. Try as I might, I could not remove those glaring yellow eyes from my mind. Ever since Winky had made his bid for freedom I had longed for another owl and so it was with great joy that I went some time later, after much scrimping and saving, with the money to buy the bird. I fully expected it to have been sold because I wanted it so dearly and because it had taken me so long to collect the cash, but my luck was in, although only just, for another falconer was preparing to exchange his Laggar Falcon for it. After seeing Walt Disney's film, *The Sword In The Stone*, I had already decided on a name for my next owl—none other than 'Archimedes', the amusing cartoon owl belonging to the magician Merlin, and so my Horned Owl was called Archimedes as well, although we usually called him 'Archie' for short.

The Great Horned Owl is found in North America and is the only Eagle Owl to be found in the United States. Archie was about buzzard *(Buteo buteo)* size and spanned just over 4 ft across the wings. His talons had an unusual cutting-edge to them, probably as an aid in grasping such elusive prey as snakes. I took him out for a manning walk and, unlike Aquila, I found him to be no bother which I considered rather unusual for an unmanned bird. His weight of 3 lb was a pleasant change from Aquila's 9 lb. I rooted out a spare bow-perch and

The glaring eyes of Archie, the Great Horned Owl.

sank it into the ground near the hedge, well away from Aquila, and fully expected the garden to be filled immediately with a seething mass of mobbing song-birds, but apart from the occasional blackbird giving vent to its alarm cries, I experienced little trouble from them. Archie was very pale coloured in comparison with Aquila; in fact, Archie was a great deal lighter in colour than all the other Great Horned Owls that I had seen in various zoological collections, for he came from Canada and the further south the geographical range extends, the darker the owls tend to become, the palest birds being found in the extreme north of the tree limits and the darkest in the southern most tip of South America.

As previously mentioned, owls have no crop and consequently I had to experiment with the amount of his normal daily food intake, but, as with most birds of prey, he ate surprisingly little and by the amount of food that remained after his daily feeds, I was soon able to calculate his requirements. I had no intention of training him until his feathers had hardened off, or become hard-penned, as it is termed in falconry parlance. He was rather vocal, especially in the early mornings when he would emit a beautiful dove-like call which trailed off in reverberated echoes. Archie often threatened me, reminding me of that trip far back in the distant past of boyhood at Thieves' Wood and the lonely ride where I had witnessed that wonderful display of the Long-Eared Owl.

Unlike my eagles, Archie was an absolute pest to rejess and I often despaired at the very thought of it, for I was usually severely bitten. I was not keen on the idea of casting him at first, with his feathers still being in the blood, and he refused point blank to lie on his back on my lap like Satan and Aquila, so it was a matter of standing him on a chairback to change them, amid the frequent swipes from his powerful black beak. One of his ear-tufts was still not fully developed, yet he perched with the developed one fully erect, threatening me with all the hostility he could muster. His quills were still very soft and he required very careful handling until they hardened off. The ideal solution would have been to have turned him loose in an empty room, but at this stage I had no such amenity at my disposal.

I wondered if he would accept pieces of meat from my fingers, so I wrapped a piece of beef in pigeon feathers and offered it to him. His large head sprang forward and snapped up the meat, including my fingers. Needless to say, I gave him the rest of the meal on my gloved fist. Archie detested anyone touching his feet. I could pat him on the head, tickle his throat locket even, but as soon as my hand went anywhere near his feet he would attempt to bite a lump out of me. I soon learned to evade his vicious beak, which eased my re-jessing problems somewhat.

A week later, Sam Barnes dropped me a line. He was puzzled by Aquila's plumage and unabated arrogance, and stated that he would call her a 'mystery' bird until he could actually come over to see her. I too was beginning to have my doubts as to whether or not Aquila was a genuine Golden Eagle. Sam went on to say that he knew of a man who flew a male Golden Eagle at hares. This eagle apparently took them well in short flights over one or two fields but if it failed to make a kill, the bird would alight on the ground and wait for its owner to pick it up. I could never envisage Aquila doing this in a million years. Despite the vast amount of time I was spending with her and for all the courses of rangling and washed meat that I lavished upon her, she remained little tamer than on the day I acquired her and she still bated away at my approach.

One afternoon, I took Archie with me for a manning walk, when a car passed me just as Archie was in mid-bate. The driver was so surprised that he ploughed his car through the front hedge of a house bordering the road. Fortunately, no one was hurt and the damage was only superficial to both hedge and car; we all had a good laugh about it afterwards, exclaiming that it was usually only mini-skirts that caused these sort of accidents, not Canadian Great Horned Owls.

I received a letter from the weekly paper *Cage and Aviary Birds* the next morning, saying that they were going to publish a section of a letter I had written them concerning 'baby-snatching eagles'. I had, of late, read several newspaper articles concerning eagles that had allegedly carried off young children, one paper even going so far as to print an article about two five-year-old boys being carried to a height of several hundred feet by two eagles, only to be released in mid-air to meet their impending doom. This sort of sensationalism prompted me to pen a rather abrupt letter, in which I naturally dismissed all these stories as journalistic rubbish; in defence I entered detailed reports of known facts concerning the lifting capacities of eagles, adding notes from my own personal experiments and observations. Thus I felt confident that I could hold my own against any possible criticism. At least I had the consolation of knowing that though mine was a small voice I was doing something constructive in defence of these noble birds.

Incidentally, I have yet to hear of a genuine case of a wild eagle attacking a child deliberately and without good cause. Regarding 'baby-snatching eagles', I wonder how many mothers are in the habit of leaving their babies alone and unattended on remote, desolate mountain slopes. It should perhaps be remembered that eagles, like most forms of wildlife, rightly shun man's presence above all else and many eagles will slip off the eyrie whilst man is a distant dot on the heather and will not return until the bird is quite certain that the coast is clear, such is their trust in mankind. At least this is the case with the Golden Eagle, at whose door the bulk of the blame is laid for alleged baby-snatching depredations.

That night, my father and I chatted into the small hours discussing the two genuses, *Haliaetus* and *Aquila*. We compared flight figures of juvenile, immature and adult birds and came to the aggravating conclusion that our Aquila was not a Golden Eagle, but, as I had of late come to suspect, an immature Pallas's Sea Eagle. This came as a severe blow to me, for it had long been my ambition to own a Golden Eagle. Eagles of the genus *Haliaetus*, a group of Sea or Fish Eagles, are generally noted for being temperamental and difficult to train, small wonder that she would not respond to the training methods prescribed by Sam Barnes for Golden Eagles. The late Captain Charles Knight, owner of the famous Golden Eagle 'Mr Ramshaw', experienced great difficulty with 'Miss America', a Bald Eagle *(Haliaetus leucocephalus)* which he brought back to England from one of his lecturing tours in the States. He had to wear a fencing mask and other protective clothing to ward off slashes from the bird's great beak.

A month later found me delving amongst the aviaries at Wilford once more, only this time the trip was to be a rather special one for me, for in one of the sheds was perched my dream-bird and ultimate goal. This fine bird was indeed a genuine Golden Eagle and I cursed my ignorance for ever supposing that my Aquila could possibly have been a representative of this species. This new bird was extremely tame and could even be trusted loose in the dealer's garden. Indeed, its former owner had apparently often kept it in such a manner. Its feet were of a vivid yellow and of immense proportions, ending in large black talons, curved like grappling hooks. The smooth, reddish-brown plumage was very dense and compact compared with Aquila's loose and untidy feathering and the Golden Eagle's tail was much longer and broader; in fact the eagle was cast from an entirely different mould from that of Aquila. Even more importantly, it was feathered to the toes. As was usual when a new bird caught my fancy, I craved day and night for it, but the dealer refused to part with it for at least a week, when two more were due to arrive from Russia.

By the following weekend I learned that the Russian Golden Eagles had finally arrived, but I was still more than interested in the other Golden Eagle which was now for sale. In order to raise the cash, I placed an advertisement in the weekly paper *Cage and Aviary Birds,* offering Aquila for sale. I had completely lost interest in flying her now. I knew for certain that she was not a Golden Eagle and in my opinion, it was not fair to Aquila to keep her tethered when someone else could be using her.

After placing the advertisement, I met an ex-army Sergeant while I was out exercising Archie one afternoon. The sergeant related that he too used to possess one of these creatures while on active service in India. Apparently, he had been able to obtain them fairly easily, 'just like Archie', he said. He went on to inform me how he used to feed his pet on bananas and found that he had to clip its toe-nails regularly. It was only then that I realised our conversation was at crossed purposes. Despite flying Archie some 20 yards to the fist in his presence, the Sergeant had literally mistaken Archie for a monkey!

One morning, I was aroused at a most unearthly hour by Bryan, my brother, who proceeded to inform me, in between shaking and prodding my immobile, prostrate form, that there were two policemen downstairs, waiting patiently to drive me to a place where an eagle had been caught and tied to an apparently frail-looking fence. I dressed hastily, removed my left shoe from my right foot and staggered down the stairs, intending to check on my own birds before I went anywhere with anyone. However, Bryan promptly informed me that he and the police had already done just that and all of my birds were sitting quietly on their perches.

By this time I was somewhere near to being half awake and slowly beginning to grasp the situation. I slipped on a warm jacket and was escorted out of the house by the policemen and bundled into the back of the awaiting patrol car. Within seconds we were speeding towards the place where the eagle was held captive. The two policemen had no real idea whether the bird was a Sparrow-hawk, Kestrel or eagle and I began to have visions of a frightened little Kestrel sitting huddled up beside the fence. But even if it turned out to be a kestrel, I would do my utmost to help it. We turned into Greenwood Road in the Colwick area and discovered that many of the local inhabitants were up and about. Practically every house was lit up, especially around the house where the bird was tethered. People were crowding the gateway, most of them clad in pyjamas and dressing gowns. We vacated the patrol car and everyone moved to one side to let me through, the police helpfully keeping the excited throng at a respectful distance.

Standing on a rock and facing me in the gloom was the largest Golden Eagle that I had ever seen. She was truly magnificent. The fence that she was tethered to could never have withstood a single bate from a bird of such dimensions, so I approached with extreme caution. But much to my surprise, she offered little resistance. In no time at all I had the bird on my fist, holding her by her jesses. I realised that she must be one of the Russian pair belonging to the Wilford dealer. The eagle was far too large to carry on my fist in the normal manner in the patrol car, so I had to carry her under-arm fashion, keeping a firm hold on both of her legs. This was easier said than done, for she bated from my fist and very nearly pulled me off balance, but I eventually had her in a position ready to go into the car. By this time, many more people had joined the crowd and

Facing me in the gloom was the largest Golden Eagle I had ever seen.

several were feeling full of bravado now that the 'savage' bird was in safe hands. With all these folk milling around, throwing questions at me, I felt like a film star and had quite a time breaking through them to the car.

The eagle insisted on my journey home being as far from comfortable as possible, and at one point, succeeded in freeing one of her feet to slash me in the chest with all her might. I felt a rib crack under the pressure and even to this day, if I happen to bend down too sharply, I am occasionally reminded of this escapade by a searing jab of pain in my rib-cage. The bird became more and more annoyed and bristled and elevated her hackles whenever I moved in a vain effort to make myself more comfortable and glared into my eyes throughout the duration of the journey.

Before long, we arrived home and I thanked the policemen for their co-operation and went indoors with the eagle, which was still protesting wildly under my arm at such undignified treatment. My father heaved a gasp of amazement as I trooped into the lounge with her and small wonder, for few other birds could have appeared a more powerful and magnificent sight than this. She spanned something in the region of 7 or 8 ft across the wings and was a beautiful dark chocolate brown all over, excluding her bright golden hackle-showered head and a snow-white tail which was tipped with a broad black terminal band, showing that the bird was in immature plumage. Full adult plumage in the Golden Eagle may take as much as five, or even six years to

Archie threatened the Golden Eagle with every display he could muster.

attain, when the tail becomes a shade of grey-brown and the white carpal patches on the wings normally recede annually until they disappear altogether.

I placed the eagle on the carpet and flopped down on a chair beside her. The huge bird puffed out her feathers until she appeared nothing short of colossal, then shook herself like a dog until her whole body rattled. The feathers then returned crisply to their former positions except for a few twisted and bent ones where I had been holding her. The magnificent creature then flew on to the back of an armchair, where she remained quietly until I completed the task of making a temporary perch for her.

As soon as the perch was completed, I carried the eagle into the garden where she sat, not on the perch that I had so carefully prepared for her, but on a large rock nearby, soaking up the few hazy rays of the dawning sun, much to Archie's dismay. He hooted and threatened the newcomer with every kind of display he could muster, for in America Great Horned Owls occasionally fall prey to marauding Golden Eagles, so I suppose Archie's reaction was only to be expected. This particular Golden Eagle rendered Aquila very scruffy-looking in comparison and entirely confirmed my suspicion that the latter was not a Golden Eagle in any way, size, shape or form. I would have given the earth to have been the owner of this superb Golden Eagle, for she far outranked the smaller one at Wilford, but I knew that sooner or later, I would have to inform the dealer of her capture, and so, dismally, I picked up the telephone

Brian Ford, ex-drummer for the late Billy Fury, also a falconry enthusiast, shown here with his favourite Lanner Falcon.

receiver and gave him the news. She was certainly his eagle and he informed me that he would come over and collect her.

I hated the thought of having to hand her over, but I had no alternative and consoled my ruffled emotions with the thought that some day the dealer might become fed up of her and sell her to me. He came round for the bird some three hours later and because he had to drive his van, I agreed to carry the eagle back to his home. It also provided me with the opportunity to observe the other Golden Eagle, which was about the same size as the one on my fist but which had an even brighter golden head. Also on the lawn with the Golden Eagle was a fine passage female Goshawk and a Mountain Hawk Eagle *(Spizaetus nipalensis)*.

While the dealer was driving me back home I could think of nothing other than being the owner of one of those two splendid eagles. The dealer had mentioned that I could have the smaller one at Wilford for the sum of £60, but it meant that I would have to obtain the cash quickly because the bird was due to be advertised the following week. After all this I was determined to sell Aquila and had a letter from Brian Ford stating that he might be able to get £50 and a Goshawk for her through a German contact.

Chapter 7

Lobo

Brian came over at the weekend, bringing with him two Goshawks and explaining that he had been breaking both hawks to the hood, although many falconers do not bother hooding Goshawks, following the popular theory that the more sights and sounds they are allowed to become familiar with, the tamer and more manageable they become. The two Goshawks arrived in a strong cage which was covered with hessian, the birds being separated from each other by a wooden partition. We placed the cage on the kitchen table and proceeded to extricate the first hawk, which was a female and a real beauty to boot. She was well over 3 lb in weight and her flaming orange-red eyes contrasted sharply with her pale grey and white plumage. The passage tiercel was considerably smaller but seemed the livelier of the pair. The choice was that I could have £50 and the tiercel, or male, or £40 and the female as she was the more valuable of the pair, so I decided on the tiercel, as £50 was almost the price of the Golden Eagle. I was to receive the balance in cash as soon as the German contact received the eagle.

Aquila was then packed into a large cage, and as soon as she was inside we covered the whole with hessian, primarily to prevent her from becoming afraid as the darkened interior would keep her quiet and still. It was quite a wrench having to part with Aquila when it came to the crunch, especially in this way and after all this time, but I had no vast fortune to inherit and it was the only way to raise the cash quickly enough. I sincerely hoped that it was all going to be worthwhile.

With the job finished and Brian Ford and Aquila gone, I turned my attentions to the Goshawk, who was eyeing me suspiciously from a bow-perch in the garden. For some now-forgotten reason, I named him 'Lobo'. He rarely bated off my fist, which is the usual habit of many unmanned short-winged hawks, but on the occasions that he did, he always clambered back on to my gauntlet rapidly, with his piercing yellow eyes practically popping out of their sockets. Although the Goshawk is taxonomically classed as a short-winged hawk, Lobo's wings were long enough to slap me across the face whenever he bated. Brian had left the hood that he had been using on Lobo, so I tried to follow in his footsteps. At the umpteenth attempt, he exploded in one terrific bate and caught a teacup on the kitchen table with one of his wings. The cup

Lobo, my first Goshawk.

hit the wall with such force that it smashed into tiny fragments. I never attempted to hood him again.

The following day, he bated from me as I entered the garden, but calmed down rapidly when I took him on the gauntlet with a small piece of meat. He tucked into this morsel heartily and accordingly, I wondered if he would jump to my gloved hand for his next piece. Taking him indoors, I placed him on top of the kitchen door and held out part of a rabbit's leg some 12 inches away from him, keeping my fist on a level with his breast, so that it made snatching at the food with his feet all the more difficult. I blew on the whistle and, much to my surprise, he was on my fist like greased lightning, pulling for all he was worth at the meat. He soon ate the rabbit and I placed him back on the door-top for another attempt. A full minute elapsed before he again came to my fist because I had allowed him to eat too much on his first 'flight', and this had taken the edge off his appetite.

As the days passed, I became aware that he was only keen to fly at a weight of 1 lb 9 oz, so I always weighed him on the scales and endeavoured to fly him at around the same time every day. If at that time I found that he was slightly overweight, I would not fly him until later in the day and would reduce his ration somewhat, for it was obvious that he had consumed too much the previous day. I had been getting him into condition for several days when I took him for a manning walk through Gedling Woods one afternoon. A rabbit bolted from its seat and Lobo was off the fist after it, only to be restrained by his jesses. How I wished he had been in full flying order, for I am convinced that he could easily have overhauled it.

A friend came to see me that same evening, bringing with him a copy of the *Nottingham Evening Post*. On the front page was an article featuring the two Russian Golden Eagles. The eagle that I had previously 'recaptured' had managed to escape yet again and was believed to be in the area of Colwick Woods. It was becoming too dark to organise an immediate search, but I went out early the following day, taking Lobo with me, as I considered it a great opportunity to put some manning in, although on reflection I have no idea as to how I could have managed both birds had I caught the eagle.

Before long, I joined forces with the dealer and we set off in his van to search for the bird. We thoroughly combed the woods but found no trace of her, so I suggested that we pay the Carlton police station a visit, in the hope that they may have received a report of the bird's whereabouts. Sure enough, they informed us that the eagle was sitting on a gate-post on the main road at Colwick. We drove at all speed to the area but, as usual, by the time we arrived on the scene, the bird had flown.

The occupants of the house who owned the gate-post, told us that the eagle had spent about four hours just perching on the white fence that borders Colwick race-course and so we visited the spot. The ironic point about all this is that the race-course is overlooked by Colwick Woods and while we had been in there searching for the bird, she was perched merrily below us, both parties being totally unaware of each other's presence. The dealer went off in one direction while I took the opposite one, hoping that by splitting up, we would stand a better chance of finding her. As dusk merged into darkness we had to abandon the search, with but one consolation; the dealer had promised me that if and when we caught the bird, he would sell her to me.

This statement gave me all the encouragement and determination I needed, and so the following day found Chris, my hawking colleague, and I at the race-course again. I assumed, rightly or wrongly, that the eagle would be flying downwind for, having nowhere in particular to go, flying into the wind and exerting herself unnecessarily would seem a rather pointless exercise. The previous evening I had plotted a course on a 1 in ordnance survey map of the region as to where the eagle would most likely be to within the nearest mile or two, taking into consideration the length of time she had already been free, distance known to have been covered and in what time, and last, but not least, wind force and direction. I predicted that the bird ought to be somewhere in the region of the great sluice gates which span the River Trent at Colwick. I prayed that the wind would not alter its course.

We took Lobo with us again and began our search on the race-track itself. This time the sky clouded over and we were soon hampered by heavy drizzle. We had covered practically no ground at all before we were soaked to the skin, but I was determined not to give up. This time I had a sort of feeling, an intuition if you like, that we would catch a glimpse of her. After a couple of hours of weary walking we still had seen nothing remotely resembling a Golden Eagle. In fact, the only consolation we had was that the rain had stopped, although the knee-high grass was still a trifle damp to say the least.

We had begun our last planned run that would take us right up to the sluice gates, when a surly character with a shot-gun beneath his arm stepped out from behind some bushes onto the path before us. He menacingly demanded that we explain why we were carrying a Goshawk on the game reserve. After a brief explanation he casually remarked, 'Oh! Why didn't you say so, it's on the bulkhead of those sluice-gates over there, been there all afternoon it has.' At first I thought he was having me on, for he said it in such a tone that one would expect it to be an everyday occurrence for an eagle to alight on the bulkhead. However, one glance in that direction revealed a dark form perched on the grass-covered island that formed the bulkhead. We made haste along the banks of the river until we drew level with the bird perched mid-stream and trained our binoculars on it. It was indeed the eagle. I handed Lobo over to Chris and, removing a large piece of tempting meat from our hawking bag, raced on ahead, leaving Chris to catch up to me in his own good time.

I was so intent on keeping my eyes on the eagle that I failed to observe a Mute Swan bathing in a muddy puddle by the river-side. I tripped full length over the unfortunate bird and joined him in his mid-afternoon bath, much to the swan's annoyance, for he promptly greeted me with arched wings and a most unfriendly hiss. Scrambling to my feet, I departed rather hurriedly and continued running until I reached the entrance to the sluice gates. No unauthorised persons were permitted access through these gates, according to the large painted sign on the gate-post, but I was determined that nothing and nobody was going to stop me now, least of all a painted sign, so I pelted full tilt across the sluice, high above the treacherous and choppy waters of the River Trent, eventually ending up on the bulkhead. I ran for the most part along the bulkhead until I came to within 20 feet of the bird. I then offered her the now rather mud-stained hunk of meat, advancing cautiously all the while.

She looked proud and magnificent as she perched in regal splendour on the tip of the bulkhead, but her leash had become entangled around her legs and feet. This made matters rather more awkward as I was half expecting the leash to be trailing behind her, so that grabbing it would have been a simple affair, but it was now apparent that I would have to grasp the bird by her legs. By this time I had approached to within three feet of the bird and placed the meat on the grass in front of her. I was puzzling the best way of capturing her when she spread her great wings and launched herself into the air, over the water and on to the Radcliffe side of the Trent, where she disappeared from view. I made a wild grab at her but missed my mark by inches and almost ended up in the river for good measure. Struggling again to my feet, I ran back along the bulkhead to rejoin Chris. I explained to him that to cross the remaining stretch of the river would entail cutting through the lock-keeper's garden, and with that, I set off again, hardly giving myself the chance to regain my breath. I ran down the garden path and shouted to an astonished lock-keeper who was busy tending his garden, telling him that I would apologise for my intrusion and rudeness on the way back. I also shouted to Chris asking him not to follow me too closely and to explain the situation to the bewildered lock-keeper. The last thing I wanted was for someone to suddenly appear on the scene while I was attempting to capture the eagle.

Once across the river, I dashed to the spot where I last saw the eagle. I had left the meat behind on the bulkhead during the excitement, although the eagle did not appear to be overly interested in it anyway. There were many gravel ponds on this side of the river in those days, although now the famous Holme Pierrepont International Water Sports Centre has been built on the site. Although the eagle was not visible, I knew that she was somewhere amongst the gravel ponds. I ran down a willow-herb infested bank and then up onto a high mound to obtain a wider view of the surrounding landscape. I still could not see the great bird, who could have been on any one of the dozens of small islands that were dotted about the ponds, although none of the waterfowl seemed unduly perturbed. Everything was quiet. So quiet that I sensed the eagle was in close proximity. I turned to face the direction from whence I had come and detected a familiar blonde head poking up above last year's dead willow-herb stalks. How I avoided treading on the magnificent creature as I had galloped down the bank is beyond me. This time I was determined not to bungle the operation.

I walked cautiously towards the bird and came to within a few feet of her when I noticed that she was preparing to take wing. In one mad, desperate leap I was upon her and finished up by slithering and rolling down the bank with her into the chilly waters of one of the ponds, striving valiantly to obtain a firm hold on the tangled leash and to avoid the possibility of being slashed in the face by her murderous talons. Eventually, half submerged, I managed to place the eagle on her back obtaining my long-awaited hold on her leash. After unravelling it, I staggered to my feet and climbed shakily back up the bank, clutching my prize tightly. Chris and the lock-keeper rushed up to see the bird and both were overcome by her size and beauty. I apologised to the lock-keeper for using his garden so rudely, but he didn't seem to mind at all and with that we left the scene, for I wanted to take the eagle home and keep her overnight as a small reward for all the trouble incurred.

The bird grabbed my bush-jacket with one of her feet and Chris was unable to free the material from her talons, even with the use of both hands, which says much for the strength of a Golden Eagle's feet. I had to carry the bird underarm fashion again as Chris was using my gauntlet to carry Lobo. In times of emergency such as this, I have always considered this method of carriage most satisfactory, and so, with the eagle still clutching my jacket, we set off down the road towards Colwick, so closing an incident that will remain indelible on my mind.

Four Kestrels flew low over our heads playing a game of tag of sorts. The Kestrels included two young birds of that year and they made a wonderful sight, but I was too tired and exhausted to fully appreciate their aerial gyrations and antics, all I wanted to do was to get the eagle home. My feet felt like lumps of lead and I continually stumbled over clods of earth and other debris which littered the journey home. When we arrived at the perimeter of the race-course Chris came up with the idea of stopping to rest at a friend's house nearby. As we neared the house the sky turned an inky black as night fell rapidly. I could only just see to tether the eagle to a secure spot in the garage, Lobo being tethered to the bow-perch shaped handle of a milk-crate.

As we relaxed in comfortable armchairs, sipping scalding hot tea, I could feel myself quaking and trembling like a leaf in a breeze from the strain and excitement of the afternoon's work. And indeed there was cause for celebration, all the hours we had spent in the mud and rain of the open fields had been amply rewarded, we had achieved our goal. Chris's friend offered us a lift back to Carlton in his estate car, and it was just as well that we accepted his hospitality, for I doubt if I could have made it back under my own steam. I cannot remember ever feeling more exhausted in all my life. On arrival home I placed the eagle in the conservatory and coaxed her into taking several pieces of fresh lean beef. For once she appeared to have given up the idea of cutting me to ribbons.

The following morning I carried her outside to a ready-made perch, but even with hessian wrapped around my wrist beneath my normal hawking glove, her talons pierced my skin like a knife through butter. I had to apply considerably more padding before she could be handled comfortably.

I had begun to fly Lobo to the fist in the garden when I had a visit from a falconer who owned a Laggar Falcon. He had come to see the eagle, for apparently news of the capture had travelled far and wide. The falconer's visit was closely followed by one from the dealer who owned the bird and once again I carried the eagle back to his house. On this occasion I also handled the other Golden Eagle which was of a much more docile temperament. After the dealer had promised to let me have the recaptured eagle for the sum of £75 I went home, elated, to relate the story to eager reporters.

News of the capture hit the headlines in the papers the following day and many local people heaved sighs of relief that it was now all over and they could safely turn their pet rabbits out to grass again without the threat of a sudden attack by a Golden Eagle. Two elderly ladies were so overjoyed when they heard the news on television that they came to thank me personally for catching the bird as they had been quite frightened (unnecessarily so) during the period that the eagle was at liberty. As for my part, I was still amazed at how accurate my prediction had been in pin-pointing the sluice gates as the probable location for the eagle and that was exactly where the bird had turned up.

Lobo was now flying to the fist immediately that he saw my garnished fist or heard the whistle. He was a smart-looking bird, this being his second year and already showing many of the barred adult feathers, especially beneath the wings, on the throat and also the flanks. His breast was a delicate shade of buff, boldly marked with vertical, tear-shaped or lanceolate dark brown streaks, while his back and wings were varying shades of grey-brown with patches of white on the wing coverts. Lobo's piercing eyes, his most striking feature, were of a yellow shade and appeared to focus slightly in the forward position, not unlike those of a harrier, or even an owl. He even had a rudimentary facial disc

Above *I had begun to fly Lobo, the Goshawk, in the garden.*
Below *The Golden Eagle's talons pierced my skin like a knife through butter, almost paralysing me.*

and his feet were huge compared with the similar-sized buzzard, being bright canary yellow and armed with long black talons. Here indeed was a true hunting bird.

One afternoon, Lobo was keen to fly and I desired to experiment by flying him to my fist out of doors from different locations. I called him from short distances only at first for the simple reason that a hawk which may respond well to flying measured distances indoors will often refuse point blank to repeat the performance out of doors, as was initially the case with Eos. Therefore, I was anxious not to undo any of his training to date by flying him at too great a distance too soon, possibly causing him to rake away and snarl up his creance in some tree or bush, upsetting the balance of his already highly strung temperament and his regard, if he possessed any at all, for me. I was fortunate, for he came straight to my fist immediately from all points as he was called, one of which was from half way up an ash tree.

One evening, I walked with Lobo on to the fields of horse-cropped grass alongside Gedling Woods to fly him at distances on the creance, a new long one, some 150 yards in length. He flew well to the fist at 25 yards and so I tried him at 50. He left the top of the post with alarming dexterity and with a few rapid wing-beats, dropped to grass-top height. He executed a short series of flaps and then glided the remainer of the way, his wicked marigold eyes looming larger and larger at his approach. He was like the shadow of death itself and I could almost experience the fear that must seize a rabbit that is aware it bears the Goshawk's deadly number. With one final upward swoop he was on my fist, pulling at his reward and shaking his tail from side to side, a truly remarkable flight. Pleased with this result, I tried him at 75 yards with the same response. I flew him once more and then the edge was taken off his appetite, but he had really earned his fill that day and I gave him slightly above his normal ration to compensate for the extra energy expended flying the extra distances.

The following evening I flew him in the same place and at the same time with similar results. Up to this point I had always flown him into wind to my fist, but I was curious to find out what the result would be should I fly him downwind. The conclusion was that he came in far too fast, hitting the glove with his hind talons with an audible thump as he overshot, turned in mid-air and returned to the branch from whence he was called. He glanced nervously about him and appeared to be rather put out, so I hastily ran upwind of him and called him off again. Since that flight, I have always ensured that any hawk of mine is always called off into wind and it has, I am sure, saved the loss of many of my hawks.

Lobo was now ready for his first flight at wild quarry. He had become very adept at grabbing a stuffed rabbit skin which was dragged along the ground on a long line, usually by a friend. I had reduced his ration on the Friday afternoon and taken him out into Trent Fields on the Saturday. He was in screaming 'yarak' (hunting mood) and glared eagerly into the hedgebottoms, occasionally giving my glove a convulsive clutch with his feet. I had not gone very far when a large brown hare got up on the opposite side of a thick hawthorn hedge I was skirting, but it scarpered into dense vegetation before I had a chance to release Lobo.

A fresh-water brook wound it's way alongside this hedgerow and thus it was a favourite haunt of moorhens. Before long I sighted four of them, probing about in the marshy ground some 50 yards ahead of me. I had already removed Lobo's swivel and leash and was holding him tightly by the jesses. I crept as near as possible to the moorhens, but was still a good 30 yards distant when they became aware of our close proximity and began creeping away, flashing their white under-tail coverts in an agitated manner. Lobo's talons gripped the glove convulsively as he caught sight of them. I raised him above my head and let him go in his own time, which was rapid to say the least. A cross-wind took him slightly off course but he soon regained himself and flew straight for the moorhens, keeping low, just above the grass-tops. Had it not been for the sound of his bells, the quarry would never have seen him until it was too late, but they spotted him before he came to within 20 ft of them.

They rose as one, two making off for a nearby bed of reed-mace and reaching it unscathed, a third headed out across the open water of a large gravel pond while the remaining bird made tracks for a distant hedge across open ground, and it was the latter which Lobo selected, much to my delight. He was much faster on the wing than the moorhen and soon caught up with it, when, for a second, I thought that it was all over. Not so however, for at the last instant the moorhen hit the ground, turned and ran for several paces, then flew back towards me. This manoeuvre momentarily puzzled Lobo and he experienced some difficulty in fathoming out where his intended quarry had got to, but he was soon in action again and, fanning his long barred tail, he turned in a wide arc and came up to the retreating moorhen at a right angle. The latter attempted its previous dodge, but this time the tactic came unstuck. The moorhen collided with a grassy mound and rolled over several times, giving Lobo ample time to secure a foot-hold and drive his talons in deeply, instantly killing it.

I made in to him on my knees and gradually covered the body of the lifeless moorhen with my gauntlet, in which I held a tempting leg of chicken. Lobo instantly stepped on to the gauntlet and pulled away at the succulent morsel while I placed the stricken moorhen in my game-bag. It was a proud moment for me, my first kill with the notorious Goshawk. Lobo was panting heavily and his wings were drooping slightly, which was hardly surprising, for this was his toughest flight to date.

I gave him an hour or so to regain himself and by mid-afternoon he had fully recovered and was still keen to fly, so I carried him across some disused sewage beds. Here we surprised a covey of partridges, or rather they surprised us, for they exploded from the ground at my feet and whirred away across the fields. Lobo was after them in a flash and was soon in their midst as they scattered and dived into any protective vegetation that came their way. I saw a puff of feathers fly up, followed by Lobo taking stand in a nearby rowan tree, where he sat for a few moments in a huff. The partridge that he struck must only have been stunned for it began to recover. Lobo came out of the tree almost vertically and crashed into the undergrowth. This time I allowed him to partake of his meal and then took him home, still plucking the remains of the partridge. I felt well pleased that I had experienced a very satisfactory afternoon's hawking.

Lobo continued to take quarry and flew well for quite some time, but it eventually became apparent that he was gradually deteriorating and he began to pant heavily after comparatively short flights. It turned out that he was a victim of a deadly infection known as *Aspergillosis*. I have since cured an external form of the latter on an African Grey Parrot using a fungicidal cream known as 'Remiderm', mixed with a carrying agent called 'Demavet'. Once daily, I had to cut back the dead tissue and smear the mixture all over the affected parts. I cut away so much tissue that there appeared a gaping hole in one wing, but gradually the infection ceased to spread and the red-raw tissue

Lobo the Goshawk, after his first moult.

healed rapidly, as did the hole in the wing. The result was a complete cure. *Aspergillus fumigatus*, one of the fungal agents which causes *Aspergillosis*, normally affects and destroys the lungs and at the present time, there is no 100 per cent cure, although there are some possibly effective treatments if the infection is detected early enough, such as the inhalation of *Amphoteracin B* vapours in a nebuliser, but even this form of treatment is known to bear harmful side-effects. So it was with the utmost grief one morning when I found Lobo dead beside his perch, stiff with rigor-mortis, so ending the career of a very fine hawk.

A falconer friend had previously borrowed one of my books on predatory birds, but I required it urgently for some reference work and went to his home to enquire if he had finished with it. However, I had a rather nasty shock awaiting me, for on arrival at his home I discovered to my horror that he had bought from the dealer, the Golden Eagle that I had so recently and so painstakingly recaptured.

The bird had been faithfully promised to me and I had been scrimping and saving for weeks on end to collect the cash, quite apart from the fact that I had parted with Aquila into the bargain. To say that I felt extremely bitter over this turn of events would be a classic understatement, partly because I now knew that I stood no chance of acquiring her and partly because of the false promises of the dealer. I tried to shake the disappointment off, but it was useless, there was no getting away from the fact that I was heart-broken. Having caught the eagle twice, I thought that I deserved first claim to her.

One morning I went to give Archie his daily meal when I discovered that he already had food of some description in his talons. His breast feathers were puffed out to such an extent that my view of the prey was obscured. I entered his shed, where he relinquished his hold of what to my amazement I found to be a hedgehog. He had neatly extracted all the flesh from inside the animal, leaving only the prickly outer shell which he had turned inside out like a sock. There were several small gaps at the base of Archie's shed which allowed passage for small animals, the only risk was of being pounced upon by a Great Horned Owl. I wondered how many more small mammals had succumbed to his talons. Archie had killed this hedgehog by instinct. He was too young to have been taught this by his parents for he was at the pre-fledgling period when I acquired him.

Some months later, I was paid a visit by the falconer who owned the Golden Eagle which should, by right of verbal and gentlemanly agreement, have been mine. He blurted out the staggering news that he now wanted to sell the bird and was I still interested. Was I! The smaller Golden Eagle at Wilford had long been sold and when the 'agreement' for the Russian bird 'fell through', I believed my chances of obtaining a Golden Eagle were nil. My only problem was that the money I had previously saved to buy the eagle had long since been used on other commodities, so once more I was low on funds at the wrong moment. It went without saying that I still desired the bird above all else, but I needed time to think the matter over and come up with the solution as to how I could raise the £75.

Chapter 8

Sable—the gentle giant from the Urals

I went for a walk on the nearby quarry to think over the situation. I already had some treasured memories of the eagle and had always believed the bird should rightly have been in my possession long ago. After much thinking and wandering over the quarry slopes, I decided to pay the eagle's owner a visit, where we engaged in a lengthy discussion over the bird's future, with the result that we came to a mutual agreement whereby I should pay him a reasonable weekly sum plus a substantial deposit. If nothing else, there cannot have been many Golden Eagles bought on HP.

I then left his premises with the eagle's ring perch, whistle and the firm promise that I could collect the bird the following evening. She was deep in the moult and had been fed almost exclusively on rabbits, which I sometimes use as a substitute for washed meat to reduce weight, therefore she had not had enough rich food to supply the feathers in blood, and consequently, there were large patches of white down where the old feathers had been shed and not replaced.

All through work the next day I felt pangs of anxiety. Would he or wouldn't he change his mind? I barely took my eyes from the clock, watching the seconds pass into minutes, the minutes pass into hours, and after what seemed like a decade, I proceeded with all haste to collect the eagle, armed with two gauntlets of varying thickness and a nylon leash. To my profound relief, the agreement was still valid, and before a change of heart could overcome the falconer, I departed with all speed for home, carrying the winged giant upon my fist.

Although she was much larger and heavier than Aquila, she was far easier to handle, for her feet were spaced well apart, one enveloping my fist and the other gripping my forearm, so distributing her weight more evenly, rather than standing with both feet on the fist. Aquila's savage temperament had given me no choice than to hold her at arms length, whereas the Golden Eagle made no attempt to slash me with either talons or beak and was of a much more friendly disposition. She bated at walls and fence-posts in a vain attempt to perch on them, but afterwards she climbed back up on to my fist with one wide sweep of her immense wings. I was out of practice with not having carried a heavy eagle for a while and had to rest my aching arm periodically by allowing her to step on to a low wall or some other suitable perch. Her feet were so powerful that they drove the talons through both gauntlets (I was wearing one inside the other) compressing the leather into my skin, leaving impressions of the seams and folds on my hand. It was obvious that I would have to make a new and much thicker gauntlet.

My father had finished the task of padding the ring-perch with hessian and it was on to this that I placed the magnificent Golden Eagle. She was out of this world in every detail and we both stood back to admire her resplendent golden head, which she held in a proud and dignified manner. I was thrilled beyond belief. After all this lapse of time and all the trouble I had incurred, she was mine at last, and as we sat and watched her preen and re-assemble her feathers I knew that she was worth every penny of the £75 that she was going to cost me.

She was a sub-species of Golden Eagle known as the Berkut, or Berkute (*Aquila chrysaetos daphanea*), the largest of all the named forms of Golden Eagle, which is found in the Himalayas, Mongolia and Siberia. The only other Berkut that I knew of in the British Isles was Atalanta, the eagle belonging to Sam Barnes in North Wales. In colouration, the Berkut is generally much darker than other races of Golden Eagle and has fine black tibial plumes. I discovered that this particular bird came from the Ural mountain range in Russia.

I kept her on a varied diet of beef, chickens, pheasants, rabbits, small birds and mammals. Her breastbone was prominent and therefore she required plenty of fresh rich food to build her up and take her safely through the moult. I exercised her daily by flying her to the fist over short distances on the quarry and after her feed would take her to the top of one of the cliffs and stand in an updraught with her. She loved this and would spread her wings wide as the wind played games with her scutulate, or emarginate, primaries. She would

Sable was much larger than Aquila but far easier to handle.

Sable never attempted to escape.

yelp and flap heavily, remaining on the gauntlet by her talon-tips, but not once did she ever attempt to fly away.

She was growing more and more new feathers every day and before long the white patches of down were almost invisible. These new feathers were of the darkest shade of brown, almost black in fact, and because of this colouration my father suggested that we call her 'Sable', after the magnificent black Sable Antelope of the African continent. The name suited her well and it stayed. Sam Barnes wrote to congratulate me on obtaining the great bird and went on to say that the heaviest Golden Eagle that he could find recorded for Scotland was 13 lb, by my scales Sable weighed almost 17 lb.

I longed for the day when I would be able to put Sable on the wing at wild quarry. I exercised her daily on the slopes of the brick quarry, which she seemed to relish, never attempting to escape when I turned her loose on the grassy hillsides. Sometimes she would gallop onto a high mound to survey the surrounding landscape, and as she stood on these mounds in all her regal splendour, it appeared to me that she felt herself queen over all. She stood conspicuous against the cobalt blue sky, with the sun's rays beating down upon her red-gold hackles, which she would elevate now and then to scratch them with one of her huge yellow feet. I believe that the only sight to excel this would be to see her in full free flight. She would already fly several yards to the fist and that was well worth watching. It reminded me of the time, many years past, when as a small boy I watched the Scottish falconer fly his male Golden Eagle in Wollaton Park. With one great downward beat from her enormous

Above *Making in to a Golden Eagle on its kill poses its own set of problems. Sable and myself on Trent Fields.*

Below *Sable mantles her kill.*

wings, Sable would leave her perch and with an upward surge, glide to my outstretched fist with graceful ease, a true symbol of power.

Making in to a falcon on the lure is no easy task for a novice. If the bird is of a nervous disposition or is at an early stage in its training and the falconer approaches in a standing position, he will probably frighten the bird, the consequences of which may well prove disastrous. The falconer must use stealth and caution when making in, especially during the early days of training. He must kneel, or crawl, if need be, up to the hawk and stop whenever it looks up and ceases to feed or shows signs of nervousness. Once it has resumed feeding, the falconer may continue. On reaching the bird and its quarry, the falconer should carefully cover the lure, or quarry, with his well-garnished fist. The hawk should then begin to feed on the meat, which should be of high quality, and as the lure is slowly pulled beneath the shielding gauntlet it should transfer its hold from lure to fist, where the jesses can be secured and the lure returned to the falconer's bag. An experienced falconer can make the switch in one careful movement and the hawk is unaware that it has been duped.

However, making in to a bird like Sable presented added problems. To begin with, eagles have a vice-like grip and jealously guard their prey, even to the point of attacking and rending their handlers on occasion. This is especially true of the Golden Eagle. Sable once stole half a rabbit from my hawking bag while I was otherwise occupied in regarnishing her ground lure. Because it had been my intention to fly her, it was necessary to retrieve the rabbit, for if she devoured it she would not be keen enough to fly. Sable however, had other ideas. She pressed her primary feathers into the earth and turned her back on me in sheer determination to keep her purloined spoils. Her beak was at ground-level and her hackles were bristling in defiance. Finally she charged, presenting both sets of fearful talons, and chased me for some 20 yards before she halted and flew back to the carcase. I decided that tomorrow might be a better day for flying and disturbed her no further, so that both our tempers should remain unfrayed.

Her powers of flight were gradually improving and she was beginning to use the wind and air-currents to her advantage. She was a sight to behold when I cast her off from the cliff-top on the quarry, rarely flying out of my sight, although she could very easily have done so had the thought crossed her mind. I am reasonably certain that it was because of her affection for me that she usually kept herself to within a radius of 300 yards from the casting-off point. On numerous occasions she would swing round in a wide arc and come in against the wind to land on my fist, and, for all her size and weight, she landed on the gauntlet like thistle-down.

I obtained a large, uncured hare skin, which I dried out by scraping off all fat and tissue residue from the pelt and pinning it to a board to dry in the sun in American Indian fashion. Three or four days later, when it had dried sufficiently, I stitched it around an old rolled-up bed-sheet which had a length of heavy-gauge wire running between the skin and the sheet to hold the latter in place and also to provide anchorage for the swivel. The swivel itself remained

*Her eyes possessed a faraway
glint in them.*

exposed at the head end of the skin so that my creance could be tied to it when the time came to introduce the contraption to Sable.

To introduce Sable to this lure, I baited it with fresh meat and allowed her to feed on it for several days. After she had become accustomed to its shape and form, I cast her off to a post in the centre of a small field and placed the lure in dense vegetation nearby. The idea was to drag the lure across her field of vision within a few feet of her perch. I attracted her attention by giving the attached creance a few slight tugs, so creating a disturbance in the vegetation. She lowered her head and glared at the rustlings in the thicket and then caught sight of the fur and the piece of meat tied between the ears which I had purposely left on the pelt. She half-opened her wings and then closed them again, staring in my direction as if to ask what on earth was I playing at. I pulled the creance sharply, so bringing the lure out of the thicket and in full view and than ran as fast as I could up the field, dragging the lure some 40 yards behind me. Sable hesitated until the lure had passed her before launching into the air. I turned just in time to see her clutch its hindquarters with one massive foot and follow up with her remaining foot which she slammed into the head end of the lure with unbelievable force. And to think that those terrible feet had, on many occasions, been mere fractions of an inch from my face.

She pinned the lure to the ground and helped herself to the small chunk of meat. After a fortnight of flying to the dragged lure, Sable became very adept at catching it and would take wing as soon as she caught sight of it. I gradually built up her strength and prowess by flying her to the fist uphill by standing on a gradient or by flying her into strong winds so that she really had to work hard to cover the 200 or 300 yards to reach me. Within a few months she was a changed bird, still friendly and amiable, but her body rippled and bulged with solid muscle and her plumage was tight and glossy following the contours of her body. Her eyes were large and round and possessed a faraway glint in them, as if reminiscing on the mountains and moorlands that were her birthright. Every morning she stood on one of her blocks, yelping and beating her wings in readiness for flight, a picture of health and vitality.

One morning, I noticed several small, pink-coloured objects moving about in one of Sable's mutes, or droppings. At first glance I thought that she was passing undigested particles of meat in her mutes, but closer examination showed them to be some type of worm. This caused no small concern on my part for I knew that many worms and other parasites could be harmful and sometimes even fatal to their hosts. These particular worms were about $\frac{1}{8}$ in or so in length and propelled themselves about in leech-like fashion.

Fortunately, my father had a colleague named Dr Iswell Watkins who resided in nearby West Bridgford and who studied nematode worms, so I packed up several of the undesirables in a plastic box and my father took them over to Dr Watkins' residence in the hope that he could put a name to them and possibly suggest a treatment to eradicate them. The 'worms' turned out to be the ripe segments, or egg-balls of a tapeworm known as *Mecosistoides perlatus*. It is a comparatively harmless species, provided that the affected bird is in good health, and is often found in predatory birds, particularly in the genus *Aquila*.

I found out from another source that the most effective treatment for tapeworms was a drug called 'Yomesan', a product of Baywood Chemicals Ltd. After a considerable amount of time and effort I managed to acquire a few tablets from a local veterinary surgeon. The dose is $\frac{1}{8}$ of a tablet per 1 lb body weight, but it is safe if *slightly* overdosed. However, I was advised to class Sable as being only 6 lb in weight and dosed her accordingly by concealing the 'Yomesan' in a piece of meat. A few hours later, I found the complete tapeworm lying in one of her mutes. It was white in colour, some two feet in length and consisted of a row of dozens of small rectangular segments. The enlarged, bulbous scolex, or head, of the tapeworm was plainly visible and on the scolex were a number of sucker-like discs with which the gruesome beast attaches itself to the intestinal wall. The treatment was highly successful, the egg-balls never appeared again, and there were no pathogenic side-effects.

Sable's performance in the bath was something of an education. First of all she would sip the water and taste it, for she eventually considered that if it was unfit for drinking, then it was also unfit for bathing in. After this initial 'sip-test', she would wade into the water until it covered her 'plus-fours' and push her head beneath the surface to raise it again rapidly, thus raining showers of water over her back and wings. She would repeat this operation several times and then puff out her plumage for a few moments in apparent ecstasy. Her next move was to roll from side to side and then backwards and forwards. After some ten minutes of this, she would jump on to her favourite perch and shake herself like a dog. She would then spend the next hour or two with her wings spread wide, allowing the ultra-violet rays of the sun to filter through her feathers and dry them more rapidly for preening.

Sable was strong on the wing now and would take the lure almost as soon as it appeared into view, although all week I had been trying in vain to catch a rabbit with her. She was taking too long to get into her stride fast enough to overhaul the quarry, and to make matters more difficult for her, most of the rabbits were but a stone's throw from the protection of their warrens. By the time I had caught up with her she was usually grabbing furiously at the hole into which the chosen bunny had safely packed his scut. Often, her entire head and shoulders would be wedged inside some of the larger burrows in one last desperate bid to make the grade.

Rabbits were rather scarce owing to a high mortality rate from myxomatosis and consequently I decided to try her at the much larger brown hare. At least, I knew that they would run the gauntlet the full length of the open fields, so allowing Sable a sporting chance. The brown hare is common in Nottingham-shire and I knew of a long grassy slope where they were abundant. On the first slip she had to battle with a strong wing which eventually proved too much for her broad sails and lifted her high into the air, finally coming to rest downwind in a tall tree on the edge of the slope. Golden Eagles use their buoyant wings for riding and soaring the mountain thermals and air currents and are not really in their element in comparatively flat English meadows, which, unfortunately, is where most English falconers see them in action and thus obtain a highly inaccurate picture of the trained Golden Eagle in flight.

I decided to leave Sable in the tree and use the advantage of the extra height to give her a better start, and with the help of a few friends I began to beat the slope in a line in order to push out the hares from their concealed forms so that they would have to run in front of her. From her elevated perch she would

I decided to leave Sable in the tree.

Sable, lucky to be alive after her tussle with a fully-grown fox.

possess the added bonus of being able to pick up speed more rapidly as she gave chase.

We had been beating for perhaps two or three minutes, heading for a russet patch in the grass some few yards distant, which we all took to be the crouching form of a hare. I signalled to my companions and could feel in my bones the tingling air of excitement and suspense that I knew we must all be sharing. What would happen next? Would it run in the right direction? Would it run at all? Would Sable chase it if it did run? What did happen next made us all gasp with astonishment, for when the animal was flushed, it turned out to be not the leggy brown hare which we all expected, but a fully grown red fox.

Old Renard bolted full tilt from his cover, his bushy tail streaming behind him. Astonishment gave way to anguish as all eyes were focused on Sable, who looked surprisingly diminutive in that vast landscape. In the Russian steppes Golden Eagles are regularly flown with success at such formidable quarry as the wolf, and, although Sable herself heralded from those parts, from her comparative inexperience, I had my doubts as to her prowess against the British red fox. She had only been flown at rabbits and hares and she was not exactly a rip-roaring success at these, so what would happen now I shuddered to think.

Sable left the bough of her tree, allowing the wind to give her more altitude until she was high above the fox's fleeing form. She then rolled over in mid-air, closed her wings and stooped in a style that would have done credit to a Peregrine Falcon. Sable was so heavy and flying at such a rate of knots that she struck the fox in the head with one, or possibly both feet, fracturing the jaw-bone on impact. The fox lay quivering in a ruffled heap in the grass as Sable began to pluck the fur from it. Despite the fact that Sable had successfully dealt

Sable was in a bad mood for the remainder of the day.

with the fox, and it had been a thrilling spectacle, she had not taken it in the correct manner and was extremely fortunate to have got away with her life.

The correct method should have meant Sable grabbing the fox by the hind-quarters with one foot, holding the other foot in reserve until the animal turned to bite, and then masking its face with the reserve, completely immobilising it and eliminating its remaining method of defence. Many a fine and valuable bird has been killed by such a faulty attack as Sable's and it has been on my conscience ever since that it could just as easily have been Sable's body lying in the grass with half her breast bitten out.

During the following week she managed to catch a leveret, or young hare, and also two rabbits, but it was the near miss towards the end of the week which gave me the most worry. Sable bated from my shoulders to give chase to a Jack Russell terrier. I had removed her swivel and leash as we were approaching the flying grounds when the dog showed itself. She chased it the full length of the road, until it sought refuge beneath a parked car. Sable pitched on to the roof of the car and then hopped down on to the road where she was only able to glare viciously at the petrified animal, for she was too large to go under after it. Every time the dog moved she tried to foot it. I hurriedly made in to her and soothed her ruffled feelings by offering her a morsel of food and, at the same time, cursed my own stupidity for allowing her to escape from my grasp.

Fortunately, few people were about and the incident went more or less unnoticed, but I began to wonder how long it would be before it became public knowledge that I was keeping a potential dog-killer. Sable was in a bad mood for the remainder of the day and refused two good slips at hares, so I returned her to the ring-perch in the garden. I would like to point out here that the

Golden Eagle will not normally tackle large animals such as dogs and foxes unless provoked or driven by exceptional hunger and I know of more than one trained Golden Eagle whose weight has to be drastically reduced to induce enough aggression to tackle larger prey. Therefore, I tend to believe Sable was the exception rather than the rule.

One morning, I received a telegram from *Reveille* magazine. Apparently, they wanted to do a story about eagles and asked if I would telephone them that evening. It turned out that they wished to do a story about my own birds of prey and asked if I would be free if they sent a reporter round that evening. I obliged. The reporters, a young couple with their son, arrived early in the evening. I had Sable in the conservatory and Archie on top of the lounge door, with liberal amounts of newspaper on the floor to catch the mutes. One of the reporters half-filled a note-pad with shorthand on falconry facts, including a page copied from one of my hawking diaries. They left some two hours later having informed me that they would be sending one of their photographers along shortly to illustrate their article.

On the appointed day I made preparations for the audition with the *Reveille* photographer. He arrived on time but we had to postpone filming for a while because the birds' plumage had been dampened by a heavy rainfall during the morning and I had to bring them indoors to dry off by the fireside so that they would not resemble spiky hedgehogs in front of the camera. Sable took the photographer's fancy and she was the first to 'watch the birdie'. After seemingly dozens of poses it became Archie's turn and he was filmed indoors. We rounded off the session with a few more photographs of Sable as I carried her in the grove outside our house. About one week later, the article appeared in *Reveille*. They gave me a full page spread which included three photographs, two of Sable and one of Archie. They also sent me 16 huge prints which were of excellent quality, plus a free copy of the magazine.

The very next day after the magazine went on sale I received a letter from a Mr Cecil Cox of Leicestershire. The envelope was simply addressed thus:

Mr D. Fox,
Eagleman,
Carlton,
Nr Nottingham.

All credit to the GPO for delivering the letter within 24 hours of its initial posting, for Carlton is scarcely what one would refer to as a small rural village. Mr Cox had read the *Reveille* article and was interested in meeting me with the prospect of viewing my birds. He had only written a brief note in the possible event that I might not receive it, because of the partial address, but he expressed a degree of anxiety that I should reply to his letter so that we could exchange information about our birds and which new species we required.

I answered Mr Cox's letter almost immediately, informing him of some of my experiences to date, and in his answering letter he informed me that he had three Tawny Owls, one Little Owl, one Barn Owl, one Eagle Owl, three Common Buzzards, one Kite, a pair of Sparrowhawks and a Raven. He also stated that I was welcome to pay him a visit any Sunday. Mr Cox wrote yet again stating that I could have his spare Tawny Owl if I required it, provided that I made the necessary arrangements to collect it. I replied to his kind offer, thanked him and informed him that I would be able to collect the owl the following Sunday. Sunday morning found me taking Archie upon my fist and boarding the first bus to Leicester. From Leicester I had to catch a second bus to the rural village of Blaby, where Mr Cox lived. I was made extremely welcome upon my arrival by Cecil and his wife.

Cecil, or Cec, as he preferred his friends to call him, was 58 when I met him, and of comparatively small build with an almost permanent beaming smile on his flushed face. I found him tremendously likeable and during what became a regular pilgrimage to Blaby, we chatted away some lengthy hours on numerous topics, often until late at night. On more than one occasion I almost missed the last bus, so magnetic and effervescent was his character.

At this first meeting I was immediately given refreshments and, after a lengthy chat, Cec showed me around his beautifully built and spacious aviaries. The Tawny Owl that I was to take back with me was in the first aviary and was in immaculate condition. We then went past a row of three large cages in which were housed a Little Owl, an immature Brahminy Kite and a Brown Fish Owl respectively. This Fish Owl was the 'Eagle Owl' referred to in Cec's letters. He didn't know what it was, for it certainly had some Eagle Owl features and colouration, was large in size and sported a pair of ear-tufts, but the bare legs, harder feathering and lack of a well-defined facial disc gave it away. I also had an advantage over Cec in that it was not the first Brown Fish Owl that I had seen.

Just around the corner, past the Fish Owl's cage was a semi-circular aviary containing a beautiful female Common Buzzard. This bird possessed an extremely aggressive nature for a buzzard and would fly at anyone who ventured too close to the wire-netting of her aviary. Cec told me that on one occasion, a neighbour's fantail dove had alighted on top of her aviary and with one upward swoop she grabbed the dove, somehow pulled it through the 1 in mesh and devoured it. With that, I cleared my throat and hastily moved on to the next aviary which housed a very nice female Sparrowhawk, the first of its kind I had seen in captivity. She had killed and eaten her mate during the week, not unlike some female spiders in habit.

Across the well-kept lawn were two huge aviaries containing a pair of Common Buzzards and a pair of Tawny Owls, the female of the pair being of the grey type. Beyond these aviaries was a shed in which a large black Raven had his domain. He was a huge bird with a beak reminiscent of a pick-axe. Cec gave this bird its food in a large enamel bowl and, after the food had been disposed of, the old Raven would wear the bowl like a hat. I used to have a Rook which could do this trick and I did not consider it to be too extraordinary until Cec handed the bowl to me—it was well over a pound in weight! In a flight near to the Raven, giving a threat display second to none, was a magnificent male Barn Owl, which thrust its head forwards and swayed from side to side, hissing loudly.

Cec and I discussed birds of prey all through the afternoon, during which he showed me how to straighten bent and twisted feathers by drawing them across the hot steam from a kettle of boiling water. He demonstrated this method using a buzzard primary feather. I could find no evidence of a crease in the quill after the treatment. I was astounded and have since turned this method to good use countless times.

As the evening drew to a close, the Tawny Owl was placed into a cardboard box and I set off for home. Cec told me that he desired any species of true Eagle Owl above all else and he confided that he was 'over the moon' about Archie, so I wrote to a Russian trapper to try to obtain a specimen of the Great Eagle Owl for him. Before I left, Cec handed me two pairs of jesses and a falcon lure made by Mr John Haywood, falconer to Twycross Zoo and whom, it transpired, was a mutual friend. I named the new Tawny Owl 'Luna', on account of his huge, orb-like eyes; he was the most attractive Tawny Owl that I have seen to this day. I put jesses on him the following morning and placed him in an aviary I had built for the purpose. He threatened Sable when she loped over to the aviary during the afternoon. Luna had been bred from Cec's true pair of owls and was wearing a closed aluminium ring on his right leg.

One morning, I placed Luna on a bow-perch to photograph him. He was perched near to Sable but no longer appeared to be concerned about her presence. A few minutes later, I happened to glance out of the kitchen window and spotted Sable plucking something on the ground beneath her perch. I detected small clumps of feathers blowing about like leaves in gusts of wind, yet I knew that she had only had a portion of skinned rabbit that morning. The feathers were brown and barred and Luna was nowhere to be seen. Fearing the worst, I raced down the garden path where my anxiety was confirmed with dreadful reality. Sable had indeed despatched Luna and was busily engaged in the gruesome task of plucking him. I pushed the eagle to one side in my anxiety, momentarily forgetting that she could just as easily have rended me as she had done Luna, but she appeared to sense that I was not playing any more and was extremely annoyed with her, so she went off in a huff to sulk on her perch.

I picked up Luna's near-naked and lifeless body which gave one final convulsive twitch and then remained still. I placed the body beside Sable's perch so that she could finish off the work she had begun, but for some strange reason she never touched it again. I wrote Cec immediately informing him of the tragedy. It was entirely my fault, for I had overlooked the fact that I had moved Sable's main perch further forward to allow her more freedom of movement. I was very upset but Sable was not to know that I hadn't put Luna there for gourmet purposes, and after all, killing is instinctive in raptorial birds.

Cec was very sympathetic in his reply, but spent most of his letter ranting and raving about Archie. He was so infatuated with the owl and had been so kind towards me that I agreed to let him have the bird. The telegram which followed my letter suggested that I should take a friend along with me to Blaby that Sunday, which was the day set to hand Archie over to his new owner. I did as Cec asked and went with a friend by car. Cec was still at work at the local English Electric factory when we arrived, but he joined us shortly afterwards.

During our visit, a man turned up with two aviary-bred, closed-rung Tawny Owls for Cec. It amazed me how successful these Leicestershire aviculturists were with breeding birds of prey. I soon discovered why Cec wished me to take along a friend, for he gave me his own true pair of Tawny Owls, which was no small sacrifice on his part, plus one of the newly arrived Tawnies, both of which were males, and concluded by giving me his female Sparrowhawk. Archie was placed on a block on the lawn and as I watched him preening, I felt very sad to be parting with him after all this time. But there was one consolation, if anyone deserved him, it was Cecil Cox, and I knew that the owl would be well cared for and that I could go and see him anytime.

The three new Tawny Owls were placed together in Luna's old aviary and settled down quite happily. The next job was to put a pair of jesses on the Sparrowhawk. Although delicate in stature, this Sparrowhawk was extremely forceful with her feet and I received several cuts before both jesses were fitted. I named her 'Andromeda' and the true pair of Tawny Owls 'Orion and Medusa', the grey phase female bearing the name 'Orion'. The odd male we simply called 'Oz'.

I was delighted with Andromeda, although her continuous bating nearly drove me wild at first. She taxed my nervous system more than any other raptor to date, but, as the days slipped by, she began to accept her new way of life and would feed unconcernedly upon my fist, indoors or out. The maintenance of her weight proved a problem, for Sparrowhawks have a delicate

Andromeda, the Sparrowhawk.

constitution and are very active little birds, whereby they burn up a lot of energy and require a higher food intake compared with similar sized raptors, such as Kestrels.

I discovered by much trial and error that if I maintained her at a weight of 9 oz, she was responsive to training. I had to be scrupulous over her feeding routine and weighed her daily on finely tuned scales which I bought especially for the purpose. It is so easy for a novice to kill a Sparrowhawk through mismanagement for they are as fragile as a china ornament and have to be treated as such, with the utmost care. Should they become too high in weight, they are lost, and too low in weight they deteriorate very rapidly, and we are talking here in terms of fractions of an ounce. Also, if incorrectly fed, they are rendered susceptible to fits, or seizures, possibly as a result of low blood-sugar levels reaching the brain and causing hypoglycaemia. And yet, having described a few of their more unsavoury traits, on the credit side, in the hands of an experienced falconer, or austringer, they are as deadly a hawk as one could wish for.

Andromeda was housed in Archie's old shed, out of the damp and draughts. Sable intently watched me put her in there and left her perch to peer round the side of the shed for a closer look. I waggled my finger at her and warned her to leave this one alone, or else; not that she could reach her anyway, so she loped off to explore some other part of the garden. Andromeda was in perfect condition, apart from a few frayed tips to some of her tail feathers. She had rufous tinges to the edges of her grey wing-coverts and mantle and her breast was an off-white, interspersed with horizontal blackish bars. She was in fact, a miniature replica of a Goshawk.

One Saturday morning, I had a most unexpected and pleasant surprise, for I received a letter from Mr Phillip Glasier. For many years I had very much wanted to make contact with this well-known exponent of modern falconry and was delighted that he had actually written to an unknown amateur like myself. Mr Glasier expressed an interest in purchasing my Golden Eagle. It transpired that Cecil Cox had mentioned Sable and her recent penchant for dog-snatching to our mutual friend John Haywood and he in turn had contacted Mr Glasier. I wrote the latter, giving him all the information on my eagle including about her being a specimen of the almost legendary Berkut. Two days later, I received his reply. He was definitely interested in the bird and wished me to telephone him to arrange a date so that he could come up from Newent in Gloucestershire to view the eagle. What on earth was I doing? Up until this point I had not even considered selling Sable to anyone. Perhaps it was because the impending purchaser was none other than the celebrated and reknowned falconer Phillip Glasier that motivated me to telephone him that evening to arrange for him to come up the following Tuesday, bringing for me a copy of his book *As the Falcon her Bells*. This was indeed an honour and a date to look forward to. But what a price to pay! As I placed the receiver back on the hook, I felt the pangs of anxiety in the pit of my stomach. I was about to complete a transaction that for me would be most regrettable, but I could hardly back out now without losing face.

Above *Sable. A front view.*

Below *Sable. A rear view showing her magnificent white tail.*

Mr Glasier arrived early in the afternoon along with his daughter Jemima, also a falconer of repute, and a young man who helped out at the Falconry Centre where they lived. Mr Glasier brought along the copy of his book as promised and had taken the trouble to autograph it for me; it is still one of the prized possessions of my extensive falconry library today. He also brought with him the largest male Goshawk I have ever seen. It was wearing a smart Falconry Centre hood and scaled well over 2 lb.

After refreshments, we all trooped out into the garden where we handled Sable, exchanged views on hawking, various raptors and the like, until we finally came to the moment that from the depths of my heart I was dreading, the business side of the proposition. As already mentioned, Sable was the very last of my possessions with which I wished to part, especially after all the palaver over her acquisition, but in truth, I was deeply concerned over Sable's recent dog-snatching escapade and I had no desire to bring the good name of falconry into disrepute. Living on the outskirts of a large city like Nottingham, as I do, could easily have detrimental effects upon the sport caused by the wrath of the local pet-keeping fraternity. Also, much of the land I had at my disposal for falconry purposes at that time was also the haunt of numerous doggies and their owners out for a country stroll and, as such, it had reached the stage where I dare not cast her off for fear of her casting her roving eye at some unwary canine.

Regrettably, the best possible solution was to part with her and use a somewhat smaller eagle, for to my way of thinking the keeping of such a magnificent bird without proper exercise, tethered to a perch, was tantamount to a criminal act. The price of £40 plus the Goshawk was agreed upon and thereby both birds changed hands. Yet I knew from the moment the transaction was completed, I would spend the remainder of my days regretting the sale of this fantastic bird. I was far from wrong.

Chapter 9

Not so much a hobby, more a way of life

So now I was in possession of another Goshawk, which I named 'Thor'. Andromeda, the Sparrowhawk, would have to take a back seat for a while until I could make Thor more amiable. His tail had been taped with gummed brown paper to protect the feathers from any possible injury during transit from Gloucestershire. While he was still in the typically demented stage of the unmanned Goshawk, I considered it to be in my best interest to allow the tape to remain on his tail until such a time as he was flying distances to the fist, for only then would he require the benefits from his fully fanned tail to act as a rudder. Ordinary brown gummed paper is ideal for this job for it is easily removed by immersion in water, thus leaving no residue of glue on the feathers, as is the case with sellotape or sticking plaster, neither of which should ever be used. I use this method as a matter of course nowadays during the earlier stages of training Sparrowhawks.

Within a few days, Thor's weight had been reduced sufficiently to calm him down and he would even jump a leashlength to my fist. His keenest weight turned out to be the 2 lb mark, almost $\frac{1}{2}$ lb heavier than Lobo's best flying weight. Inside a fortnight he was flying long distances to the fist, even out of trees.

I also managed, by superhuman effort, to keep Andromeda fit and flying and she made her first kill one morning as I was carrying her down the garden to her bow-perch. She had bated at a couple of starlings which were feeding at the bottom of the garden and which, despite Andromeda's bate, still had not seen us, so I slipped off the leash and swivel and held her up. She waited, poised like an arrow in a bow at full draw. Nothing much was happening so I let out a muffled cough, causing the starlings to take wing. Andromeda was off the fist in a flash and took the laggard one as they nipped over the garden wall into the farmland beyond. She bound to it in mid-air and I found her some five minutes later, beneath dense undergrowth, on her partially plucked kill.

As with Sable, I made a ground-lure out of a dried rabbit skin and introduced it to Thor, the Goshawk. Thor, however, was never very keen on this contraption and flew it with very little zest. Neither would he fly enthusiastically at rabbits that I flushed for him on numerous occasions, several of which he should have taken with comparative ease. It was some weeks before I discovered the problem. I had been walking up a rough, bracken infested hillside, still trying for rabbits, when a cock pheasant broke cover and whirred away down the hill. Thor came alive and tore down the hill after it, taking it before it had covered barely 100 yards after a superb tail-chasing flight. He was depluming it with fury when I made in to him and he mantled over his prize in a bid to prevent me from depriving him of his spoils. When that failed, he attempted to carry it, so I allowed him to break well into it and take half a crop before taking him up.

Unfortunately, at that time I had very few available flights at suitable feathered quarry and so I persevered with the rabbit ground-lure. Thor caught a half-grown rabbit on one occasion but released it and returned to the gauntlet. Obviously, he had a marked preference for feathered game. Never before or since have I come across another Goshawk quite like him. Flying him at quarry became a rather frustrating affair. I was despairing when I put up rabbit after rabbit and he refused each one time after time. Eventually, I stopped flying him, for even continuous use of the ground-lure failed to improve his performance at rabbits.

However, to compensate, I had great sport with Andromeda on Trent Fields, flushing birds out of hedges and bushes, during which time she caught several, ranging from sparrows to a partridge. On one occasion she even took off after a Mallard Drake which eventually made its way to a gravel pond and sought refuge in the protective cover of a reed-bed, although I doubt very much if she could have held it for very long had she caught it. She was a game little hawk and I totted up a number of kills with her before she was tragically executed one night by a marauding cat. I had been away from home all day and the hawks had to remain outside for part of the night until I could return to move them under cover. All that remained of Andromeda was a number of pretty, barred feathers which trailed off into the hedgebottom; her legs and feet were still attached to the jesses, swivel and leash, the latter still being held securely onto the ring of her perch. The cat had pulled her legs completely out of their sockets as he dragged the hawk away. A sad end indeed to the career of a very fine hawk. Of course, it was all my fault. I should never have weathered them that day, for I was reasonably certain that I would be late home. Steep is the price paid for experience. It was one of those cases when one always seems wiser after the event; if only we all possessed foresight. Thor was passed on some time later to a colleague in Salford who had access to large quantities of feathered game, at which he proved himself a deadly adversary.

I had always had a yearning to breed birds of prey in captivity so I built a large nest-box in the Tawny Owls' aviary and, to my delight, Orion used it immediately. Within a few weeks, Medusa would launch an attack upon anyone who entered the aviary to approach the nest-box. This was my first attempt at captive breeding, a subject which I 'was soon to turn into an obsession, and I had high hopes of breeding from the pair. Cec was very interested in the proceedings and asked to be kept informed, maintaining that they had bred the previous year following such displays of ferocity. They called incessantly throughout the night and I feared complaints from the neighbours,

but luckily, no one seemed to associate the racket with my owls and even if they
did, they said nothing about it.

All through the spring and early summer I kept a sharp watch on the owls as
they took turns to use the nest-box, then one day they both abandoned the
practice and sat out in full sunlight on a branch. I was rather puzzled by their
apparent change in behaviour and finally entered the aviary to determine the
cause of it, fully expecting one or the other of them to have a go at me. But they
simply sat and stared, then turned away altogether, totally disinterested. This
was indeed a transformation from their previous behaviour. The nest-box was
found to be devoid of anything remotely resembling Tawny Owl eggs or owlets
and they were now using it to store their food. I pondered the situation,
wondering if they had laid earlier in the season, hatched the young and then
eaten them. I had resisted the temptation to check the nest earlier in the year on
account of their repeated attacks, believing that they might have deserted had I
interfered. So ended another mystery to which I shall probably never know the
full answer. How I wish I had made a quick observation of them earlier to
determine that eggs had at least been laid.

In the meantime, I had made the acquaintance of Ian, a Glasgow-born
veterinary surgeon who was employed at a practice in Nottingham. He was
interested in falconry and had seen the *Reveille* article while he was still in
Scotland. Ian had desired to see Sable in action so much that I told him about
Sam Barnes and Atalanta in North Wales. He was keen enough to go the
following weekend, taking me with him.

Ian arrived early in the morning so that we could spend most of the day with
Sam. He was driving an Anglia estate car of some vintage and he doubted its
ability to get us there and back, but luckily, the old girl served our purpose
well. The journey to Pwllheli was a long and arduous one, though not entirely
uneventful. We spotted five buzzards on the soar from a Welsh mountain road.
The road was only wide enough for one car and there were passing places every
half mile or so, but these buzzards were floating about on the thermals well
away from the nearest passing place, so we halted on the spot and jumped out
of the car to obtain a better view of their aerial manoeuvres as they soared way
up over the pine-clad slopes. Shortly afterwards, we became acutely aware of
much car-horn blowing and blasts of abuse from unornithologically minded
drivers who were forced to pull up behind us. Ian garbled something at them in
his native Gaelic and we drove on, passing through Dollgellau where we saw a
wild Merlin skimming over the heather strewn moors, then across the
Portmadoc sea-wall, on to Criccieth and finally to our destination, Pwllheli.

I entered a hotel to enquire as to where I might find Mr Sam Barnes and was
greeted with a series of Welsh double 'l's', which for the most part went clean
over my head. However, one kind lady was able to direct me in decipherable
language and we presently located Sam's hotel, which was situated on the
promenade, only yards from the sea. Sam was scantily clad in a pair of bathing
shorts and elegantly spread-eagled over the front lawn, soaking up the sun
when we descended upon him. He disappeared indoors to make us a pot of tea
while I glanced at various familiar falconry articles scattered about the front

Sam Barnes with Atalanta and Shep outside his hotel in Pwllheli, North Wales.

garden; but the main object which riveted my attention was a huge, sawn-off tree trunk, which Sam later informed us was part of the trunk of a banana tree. Sam could tell from my vacant expression that I could not imagine why he should choose a banana tree of all things for Atalanta's perch, so he went back indoors and emerged some seconds later with a large pan of water which he poured over the trunk. I was astounded. The water immediately soaked right into the wood, leaving the splashed surface bone dry, making it useful in rainy weather. Below the trunk were remnants of some of Atalanta's meals. I picked up the dried remains of the long-beaked head of a guillemot which Atalanta had killed on her way in from some sortie in the mountains and had carried home to devour.

Which brought us to the subject of Atalanta. Where was she? Sam told us that she had been away since early morning, but assured me that we would go and look for her later on. Sam could see that we were somewhat disappointed and Ian suggested to me in confidence that she might really be in the basement of Sam's hotel, for, after all, a homing Golden Eagle does take some swallowing. I must confess that I too had my doubts, but in the meantime, to compensate, Sam showed us dozens of photographs of the well-known eagle on many of her exploits.

Early in the afternoon, Sam donned more suitable attire for the mountains, which we could see from the sea-shore in front of 'Wavecrest', Sam's hotel. They were just a blue haze on the horizon, but Sam said that Atalanta was over there somewhere. A couple of doctors and colleagues from the neighbouring hotel joined us and before long we set off for the distant mountains in a convoy of three cars. We halted on various high vantage points but could see nothing in the way of a Golden Eagle, although the scenery was breathtaking. Temporarily abandoning the cars, we made our way on foot over the mountains to a spur of land above Bardsey Sound on the most north-western tip of Wales. Here, the dark, perpendicular cliffs plunged hundreds of feet down into a crystal-clear sea, whose breakers crashed unceasingly against the cliff walls.

Across the sound loomed the large, dark and uninhabited island of Bardsey, upon which there is a bird observatory. It was certainly in the right place, for birds of many species abounded everywhere. Cormorants, like large black sentinels, perched precariously on pinnacles of rock which jutted out from the base of the cliffs. A Shearwater skitted across the surface of the water towards Bardsey, flying so low as to become almost engulfed by the waves. Hundreds of gulls wheeled in and out of the thermals and Rock Pipits flitted all over the place. But my first surprise came when I spotted what I at first thought to be a Kittiwake on its nest. I climbed down to the ledge below the nest and to my sheer delight found the bird to be a Fulmar Petrel, somewhat resembling a pocket-sized version of an albatross and the first of its kind that I had ever seen. The bird was so tame that I was able to place my hand upon its chest without it taking fright. However, when I shifted to a more comfortable position, I was rewarded with a squirt of what appeared to be cod-liver oil, but Sam later told me that Fulmars often discharge this fluid from their nostrils when disturbed by intruders at the nest site.

I ventured further along the cliff-top where I saw two large black birds flying across from Bardsey to the mainland. They flew out of my field of vision and alighted behind a huge boulder some 50 yards in front of me. I could have sworn that I had detected the long, curved, orange beak of the Chough, a member of the crow family and one of the rarest birds in the British Isles, which formerly bred in Cornwall but now inhabits a few stretches of the rocky Welsh coastline. I trained my binoculars on the boulder and within a few moments, out stepped a Chough. I was elated, as I had never before seen one outside of a zoo. This alone made my trip to Wales worthwhile. But it didn't end there, for a total of three pairs of Choughs nested on the cliffs of Bardsey Sound which, fortunately for the Choughs, is National Trust land, and later in the day, I found one of these nests containing four gaping-mouthed young.

We ambled over the heather-covered hills putting up several hill foxes and even found a Ring Ouzel's nest in a gorse bush at almost ground level. I only saw the cock Ring Ouzel, looking very much like a blackbird except for his white chest 'ring'. We left the Ring Ouzel and followed a rough sheep track down to the sea where Sam introduced us to a strange phenomenon, known locally as St Mary's Wells. These wells are underground springs which come up into the sea causing something which resembles a whirlpool on the surface. All around these whirlpools was salt-water, yet the pools themselves were composed of saline-free refreshing mountain stream water and local legend has it that this water has holy properties. Several members of our party seemed convinced and bottled samples of it for souvenirs; and I my self partook of

Sam took Atalanta on the beach and flew her for me.

some, for, after all, there is often a ring of truth in some of these old legends.

We started back up the steep mountain paths, leaving Bardsey behind with deep regret, for its dramatic scenery and birdlife had almost made up for not finding Atalanta. The mountain roads were narrow and winding and we followed them for several miles before we came to a halt outside a stone cottage, whose outer walls were encrusted with yellow-flowered Biting Stonecrop and fleshy-leaved Wall Pennywort. We went into the cottage where Sam introduced us to his friend, the poacher. He was an ageing man and what he didn't know about the local wildlife just wasn't worth knowing. The cottage walls on the inside were adorned with a variety of traps, snares, stuffed animals and skins and was an antique collector's paradise. Sam had set the poacher with the task of catching one of the local white variety of the brown hare which Sam required to mate with his own captive white hare, 'Eidelweiss'.

By the time we arrived back at Sam's hotel, the sun was low in the sky and still we had not seen Atalanta. Ian suggested that we begin to make tracks back to Nottingham, for he had a surgery in the morning, but Sam insisted that we stay for a pot of tea. We agreed, and while he went indoors to brew it, I strolled along the promenade and was looking out to sea and across the bay to the far distant mountains, when a shout from Ian made me whirl round just in time to observe Atalanta soaring across the bay and over the roof-tops with hardly a wing-beat, to land on the banana tree in Sam's front garden.

There is but one word to describe the event, incredible. I raced back along the promenade to the hotel where the huge bird sat preening her feathers. She was almost identical to Sable except that she was in adult plumage. I used up an entire film on her and after tea, we took Atalanta on the beach and flew her. She wore no jesses although Sam always carried a pair with him. So now I had seen her, the only homing Golden Eagle in the British Isles. I was disgusted with myself for ever doubting Sam's words. The locals knew Atalanta well and never raised a gun at her, but the end result would be quite the contrary in the industrial Midlands, where she would be shot on sight within a week.

It was almost dark when we left Pwllheli and we were very low on petrol. The fuel gauge needle was on the empty mark and we were still 18 miles from Shrewsbury, all the local garages being long-since closed. We drove uphill and then switched off the engine to roll down hill to conserve petrol until we ran out totally at a closed garage some three miles from Shrewsbury. We hammered upon the door of the house adjoining the garage, despite the fact that it was 3 am. A large Alsatian guard-dog howled at us from its netting compound at the side of the building and we were on the verge of preparing to spend an uncomfortable night in the car on the garage fore-court until morning when an upstairs light flashed on. Presently, the hall light came on and into view through the glass door came the garage attendant, still clad in night attire. Understandably, he was somewhat irate and cursed us for disturbing his dreams, but after threatening to unleash his dog upon us should we dare to disturb his slumbers again, he obligingly filled our petrol tank. We scarpered down the road before he had second thoughts about exercising his overgrown dog.

One afternoon, after picking up my copy of *Cage and Aviary Birds*, my mother read out aloud one particular portion of that week's obituary column, a portion which stunned me to near oblivion. It is perhaps more satisfactory to record it here as it was printed in the paper:

Mr C.E. Cox, Blaby

It is with deep regret that I report the death on Sept. 24th in a motoring accident of Mr C.E. Cox of Blaby, Leics. Aged 58, he was a life-long fancier and well known as a breeder and exhibitor of British birds. Recently he had built up a collection of Birds of Prey. A true fancier, he was always willing to help others with stock or help them to build quarters for their birds. D.G. Sturgess.

I snatched up the paper. It couldn't be true. I refused to believe it. Cec just couldn't be dead. The matter was just too preposterous to contemplate. I wandered vacantly down the garden path, fighting back the tears. I sat down next to Lady Jane Grey, a buzzard which Cec had so kindly given to me on a recent visit and spoke softly to her, 'Our old friend is dead Buzz, we shall never

Lady Jane Grey, the Common Buzzard. A gift from the late Cecil Cox.

see him again', and with that I sank to my knees with my head buried in my hands, stricken with grief until finally, I could fight the tears back no more and broke down.

Cec was one of the few members of the human race that I had absolute and total respect and admiration for. He had done so much to help me with my birds and on many an occasion I benefitted greatly from his help and advice. He took life in his stride and I cannot recall ever seeing him without a smile on his face; he was the most cheerful soul I have ever met. To me, his passing marked the end of an era, and I have never been able to find anyone quite like him since.

Cec had been dead and buried for a full fortnight before I knew anything about it. I took the next day off work and went to Cec's house, praying that it was a misprint and was not true, but of course it was. Mrs Cox was at work to try and help her overcome her tragic loss and a neighbour informed me that Cec's collection had been removed by our mutual friend John Haywood and taken to Flamingo Bird Gardens at Olney in Buckinghamshire. There seemed to be nothing I could do now, so I posted a note through the letter-box expressing my deep sorrow, but only my parents really knew just how much feeling had gone into the writing of that note.

Dismally, I caught the next bus back to Nottingham, feeling as though the bottom of my world had fallen through. I arrived home to discover a letter from Cec's daughter, explaining in detail the cause of his death. Cec had always ridden a moped, but had recently bought a larger motor-bike, against all our wishes, and had been riding this new machine to collect a consignment of day-old chicks from a local hatchery for use as food for his birds. He had pulled up at a cross-roads near Wigston in Leicestershire when a car drove straight into the back of him. Having little or no protection on a motor-bike, Cec stood very little chance and was found to be dead on arrival at Leicester Royal Infirmary. To this very day, I have still not fully overcome my grief at the loss of such a dear friend.

The local rabbit population, not to mention moorhens, rats, squirrels and the like, were becoming more and more wary of trained hawks. Kills were becoming few and far between, so I came to the conclusion that I would have to accept the invitations of various colleagues to hawk their lands much further afield. The only drawback was transport, or lack of it. This was overcome when a friend informed me of an aged mini saloon car for sale at a local garage. It was in fair condition for all its antiquity so I bought it, persuading a friend to drive it home for me, as I couldn't drive. However, that problem was also overcome, for within six months, and much to my surprise and delight, I passed my driving test at the first attempt. Now I was mobile, with the power to take my hawks to all the remote corners of the country.

Shortly after the tragic death of Cec Cox, I was offered a Goshawk from a falconer residing in Barnsley in Yorkshire. Terry Hibberd, the hawk's owner, was sitting on a wall outside his home when I drew up in the car, but soon welcomed me into his home and eventually down the garden path to his mews, where sat the largest female Goshawk that I had ever seen in my life. She was almost as large as a Bonelli's Eagle (*Hieraetus fasciatus*) and the only reason for the sale was that Terry wanted to buy a certain car and to help pay for it he would regretfully have to sell 'Rudi', the Goshawk. Rudi scaled an almost unbelievable 4 lb 1 oz and had originated from Scandinavia. Her feet were of tremendous dimensions and I had high hopes of an exciting forthcoming season. She came into 'yarak', or hunting condition, at 3 lb 12 oz, a whole pound heavier than the usual flying weight of the average female Goshawk.

Rudi had barely completed her training programme when I took her hawking with a colleague who also owned a Goshawk. My friend had hawking rights on some farmland at the tiny village of Thrumpton, near Ratcliffe on Soar. The farm runs parallel with the River Trent, but we steered well clear of the river for recent heavy rains had turned it into a surging torrent of frothing brown water with no bridges either way for miles; the thought of a possible kill on the opposite bank made us both quail. Both hawks were slightly above normal flying weight and my bird was only on her 11th day of reclaiming and I was still unsure of her disposition. We forded a shallow stream and walked along its muddy banks, hoping to flush a few rabbits; but nothing stirred. In fact we saw precious little until I spotted a Carrion Crow playing about in the middle of a field. I cut through a gap in the hedge surrounding the field and held Rudi above my head at full arms-length. She didn't appear to be too clear in her mind as to what I expected of her, but suddenly, she convulsively gripped my glove and I let her go. Disappointingly, she flew directly over the crow's head and took stand in a tree on the far side of the field. I ran towards the crow waving my arms about and attempted to get it to take wing, but I believe it was unwell, for it fluttered and floundered into the hedgebottom close to where Rudi had taken stand. Rudi finally saw it and dropped like a

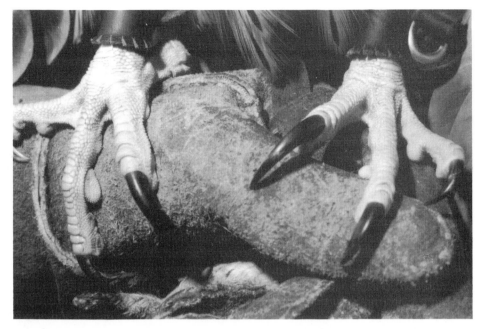

Above *Rudi's feet were of tremendous dimensions.*
Left *Rudi the Goshawk was almost as large as a Bonelli's Eagle.*

stone into the hedge. On her 11th day of training, Rudi had made her first, if somewhat unstylish, kill.

Then Rudi suddenly developed the terrible habit of screaming. It was an ear-splitting and irritating sound which forwarned all rabbits to beat a hasty retreat and to pack their white scuts into the safety of their warrens. Obviously, my much-loved Goshawk had been removed from the nest as a very small eyas and had become partially imprinted on the human form. All it required to start her off was the weight reduction necessary for training and I was now suffering for it, missing many slips on account of her ever open maw.

My hawking colleague at Thrumpton joined me for another hawking trip on Trent Fields. We covered a lot of ground but found nothing to slip the hawks at. All the signs showed that rabbits were in abundance, but suitable slips for the Goshawks were few and far between. It was almost dusk and we had practically completed our beat when I noticed a rabbit running down a bank across the open field towards a large wood which fringed the River Trent. I cast off Rudi and she gave chase, closing the 100 yard gap at a terrific pace, but the rabbit reached the safety of the wood and Rudi threw up into a tree just inside the leafy canopy. Then, just when I thought the flight was over, I heard the tinkle of Rudi's bells as she dropped from the branch to crash headlong onto the ivy-covered woodland floor some 50 feet further into the dense wood. I heard a scuffle on the floor then all was silent, the wood fell into a deathly hush. I scouted around for a while but could see nothing of my hawk until I caught

Above left *Rudi developed the terrible habit of screaming.*

Left *I caught sight of Rudi's sharp yellow eyes blinking amongst the undergrowth.*

Above *Myself with Rudi the Goshawk and Jemima Glasier with her Laggar Falcon at the Nottingham Festival, Woolaton Park.*

sight of Rudi's sharp yellow eyes blinking amongst the undergrowth and found her mantled over the rabbit, up to the neck in vegetation. She had made a good clean kill at last.

On the eve of the first ever Nottingham Festival, I took Rudi along to watch a falconry demonstration which was being held in Wollaton Park as part of the festival programme. A female Laggar Falcon was flown to the lure by Miss Jemima Glasier, daughter of Mr Phillip Glasier who had purchased Sable from me. After the demonstration, I flew Rudi to the fist at the rear of a long row of tents. She flew well twice, but on the third and final flight, an unforeseen group of mounted mediaeval knights in armour clattered across the path to her rear, causing her to take fright and flight. She flew off at great speed to alight in a large horse-chestnut tree some 200 yards distant. I attempted to bring her down to the ground-lure but she was only mildly interested and after a few minutes she moved off downwind and was lost from view for a time until one of my companions discovered her in another tree. As soon as I appeared on the scene she vacated this tree also and sailed into a large copse. I heard her bells and found her, high up in the crown of a massive elm tree on the far side of the copse. She was on the ourskirts of the park by this time and it was growing dark, so I purposely flushed her in order to make her fly back into the park centre and marked her down in a smaller copse where she had obviously decided to spend the night. We failed to locate her exact position in the gathering gloom but I planned to return the following morning at first light, notifying the mobile police wagon of my intentions on my way out of the park.

A fellow falconer who had been with me when Rudi did her vanishing act the previous night, arriving at my house at 4:30 am the following morning. I had spent an uncomfortable night on the sofa for I had no wish to oversleep as I was sure that Rudi would move off elsewhere with the arrival of dawn. Shortly before 5 am, we found ourselves scaling the walls surrounding Wollaton Park in true commando style where, once over, we split up to cover both sides of the copse. We dragged ground-lures and blew whistles, but Rudi failed to put in an appearance.

Then I heard the 'pinking' of blackbirds and other song-birds in a wood by the lake-side, but on investigation, the fuss was over nothing more than two fluffy baby Tawny Owls perched side by side on a branch near the top of a large beech tree and only yards from the clump of yew trees which had provided the daylight roost for a pair of Tawny Owls in my early youth. As the hours ticked by, I had to continue the search alone because my colleague had to return to work, for, as luck would have it, I was on holiday. The sun was at its brightest and the summer heat became oppressive. Flies pestered me all morning and the meat that I had tied onto the lure soon became dusty and fly-blown. Rudi had seemingly vanished into thin air and so eventually, I returned home.

The escape was well publicised and I soon received several telephone calls, one coming from a man who claimed to have seen her by the 17th green on Wollaton Park golf-course. I returned to Wollaton Park and spent the afternoon combing the 17th green and surrounding area up to Derby Road, but again without success.

The next day I had a visit from the police who informed me that Rudi was at my former place of employment, the horticultural research station at Lenton (I had since joined the staff as senior technician in the Department of Cancer Research at Nottingham University), which lies just across the road from Wollaton Park. A colleague who was still employed there had been out shooting wood-pigeons and had hit one during the course of his outing, sending his young son to retrieve the carcase. The boy returned shortly afterwards empty-handed, exclaiming that an eagle was sitting on it! He had been able to approach to within two yards of it before Rudi flew off into the trees behind Lenton House. I borrowed a powerful torch and searched the trees throughout the remainder of the night and half the next day. But it was all in vain, Rudi was always just that one wing-beat ahead of me.

Five whole weeks after the dramatic loss of Rudi during the Nottingham Festival, I heard the unbelievable news, by telephone from a friend, that Rudi had been captured and was on the ring-perch in the garden of a colleague. She was caught at Boots the Chemist's warehouse near Beeston by my friend who

Rudi was deep in the moult after her spate of liberty.

Rudi was deep in the moult after her spate of liberty.

succeeded in hooking one of her jesses with a piece of bent wire and managed to hold her thus while he climbed up and grabbed her as she sat on the bough of a tree. I could scarcely believe my good fortune and went to see her almost immediately. Sure enough, the rascal sat there as large as life on the ring-perch. After five weeks of intensive searching she was finally in my possession again.

She was deep in the moult and very loose feathered but she had maintained her normal flying weight, indicating that she had been killing on a regular basis during her weeks of unintentional 'hack'. Her beak and talons were overgrown but a quick coping operation soon remedied that. A longer job turned out to be the curing of an attack of Frounce, which covered her tongue and parts of her mouth and throat with a whitish coating resembling the calcium deposits or 'fur' lining the insides of old kettles and which was undoubtedly contracted from eating pigeons, for it was known to me that she had killed several of them during her spate of liberty. I used the drug 'Emtryl' and dosed her with one tablet daily for 14 consecutive days, whereupon the infection cleared up completely.

Soon afterwards, Rudi was strong on the wing again and I took her along to the Stapleford Lion Reserve near Melton Mowbray in Leicestershire where I had been invited, along with other members of the East Midlands Hawking Club which I had recently founded, to put on a flying demonstration as part of a country fair being held in the reserve grounds.

I had an innate fear of Rudi taking stand in one of the trees behind a nearby wire barrier, not because the trees were unscalable, but because there were half a dozen fully grown lions stretched out in the shade beneath each one!

Fortunately, no such adventurous events took place and the demonstration went without a hitch. We were joined there by a Sergeant David Symons of the Royal Army Veterinary Corps who was stationed at the remount depot at Melton Mowbray. He had recently returned from a spell of duty in Hong Kong and he and I immediately became firm friends. The day after the display at the lion reserve I called on him, at his invitation, to view his birds, for he too was a falconer. I discovered that, because of his large build, Sergeant Symons was known affectionately to his friends as 'Slim', and with his kind permission, I will refer to him thus henceforth.

Slim had been interested in falconry for years and had his first opportunity to practise the sport while stationed in Hong Kong. He frequently watched Bonelli's and Imperial Eagles on the soar, sometimes both species being seen together. Peregrines too were fairly numerous. He failed to trap any, however, and had to rely upon the local bird shops for his charges. Apparently, the Chinese generally regard hawks as nothing more than candidates for the cooking-pot and believe that the consumption of an eagle will give a man greater longevity, on account of the eagle's own long life. Consequently, the shops and bazaars were full of various hawks, falcons and owls for culinary purposes.

On his return to England, Slim, together with an Army Captain, managed to bring back a pair of Bonelli's Eagles, a pair of immature Imperial Eagles and a minute passage tiercel Peregrine, quite the smallest of its kind I have ever seen and which also possessed a remarkably rich-coloured breast. Only one of the Bonelli's Eagles actually belonged to Slim, the Captain eventually selling off the remainder to prospective buyers up and down the country. Slim's Bonelli's was unique in that apart from having 13 tail feathers instead of the usual 12, one of these was pure white and every year it moulted out and regrew albino. I have one of these unusual feathers in my collection. His bird was housed on the Army camp, with the Colonel's blessing, in a converted former 'wive's clubroom', which provided for a very spacious mews. The eagle, whose name was 'Wong-dai', meaning Emperor in Chinese, was deep in the moult and not flying, but Slim was looking forward to putting him through his paces. Before I left I obtained a good series of photographs of all five birds on the camp.

Nottingham University had granted my father a house near to the campus at Dunkirk on the southern outskirts of the city. We spent a whole day moving there from Carlton. By 3 am the following morning, the only possession of ours left in Carlton was my Goshawk, Rudi, and I made a special last journey to collect her. This new house was an improvement from all points of view, especially mine, for it was equipped with two spacious lawns and a brick out-house, which I rapidly converted into a mews.

The weekend after moving house, I joined Slim at Melton Mowbray where we sought after quarry with Rudi and Wong-dai, the Bonelli's Eagle. In a shallow valley behind the stables at the remount depot lies a reservoir, which for the most part is choked with weeds and shrubbery, but is a natural haven for the moorhens which abound there. Now, a moorhen in the chalk-streams counties and other such open areas is often too easy a quarry for the average

Wong-Dai, Slim Symons' Bonelli's Eagle.

Goshawk, but in this jungle of weeds it is a very slippery customer indeed and despite the fact that we have extensively hawked it over the past few years, only five moorhens have actually been taken. The first one ever to go into the game bag was taken by Rudi.

Slim and I had beaten most of the cover on the reservoir and had sent the bulk of the moorhens scurrying for cover towards a small, bush-fringed pond on the top of the rise on the opposite side of the valley. They had to make a break for it over an open field to reach the pond, but when they did eventually flush, I was too badly placed for a slip and the Bonelli's was none too keen on chasing moorhens anyway. We crossed the stream which fed the reservoir and made a bee-line for the top pond, Slim on one side and I on the other. A moorhen was flushed on Slim's side of a row of trees which flanked the pond and made it back to the safety of the bottom reservoir again, out of sight of Rudi's prying eyes. A few yards further on we surprised a second moorhen, this time on my side. It gained a good 30 yards lead on us as I cast off Rudi. With hardly a sound except for her bells, she speared her way through the air and caught up with the moorhen in seconds, fetching it an almighty clout while still some 20 feet in mid-air, sending up a flurry of black feathers. The remainder of the flight was obscured by a large hawthorn bush, but suffice it to say that I raced across the coarse grassland to find Rudi beneath the bush, clutching her prize tightly in her gnarled yellow feet. The moorhen was as dead as a doornail. I made in to Rudi and she quietly stepped onto my garnished glove. Then, without warning, as I was extricating the pair of us from the tangled, thorny boughs of the bush, Rudi struck at my face with her feet, catching me in the right nostril with her huge, left inner talon. The inflicted wound was deep and bled profusely, but all I could do was to continually wipe away the blood and carry on hawking.

Many of our hawking forays fail to result in kills and, perhaps surprisingly, some of my most memorable days have been full of exciting flights, all ending in failure. It is the privilege of being allowed a ringside seat to watch a natural drama that the vast majority of normal bird-watchers can only dream about, for the chances of seeing a wild hawk kill are somewhat remote. Only with Ospreys and Fish Eagles which regularly hunt a particular lake does the watchful observer stand any real chance of recording a kill, for in other species prey is killed away from the nest, often in deep cover, and is already dead when brought in to the incubating female. Also, to return to hawking, the quarry which escapes on one occasion is unharmed and will be there for another day. One such exciting event follows thus.

I had organised a full club field meeting which took place one morning in autumn on Trent Fields. The fields were bronze with sun-bleached stubble and there had been a slight ground frost which mingled with the clinging mist that drifted off the choppy waters of the River Trent and rolled and wafted its way across the fields like liquid nitrogen. But this soon lifted as the cheerful sun broke through a barrier of heavy cloud. We had a good turn-out of members and also had a ferret, a black labrador and a springer spaniel in addition to the hawks, which included three Goshawks, a buzzard, two Laggar Falcons, one Lanner Falcon and the Bonelli's Eagle.

As we entered the fields, George slipped his Lanner at a flock of feral pigeons, but she showed little interest in them, having only just regurgitated her casting. She was brought in to the lure and we made for some rough ground which I call 'the pheasant land', for obvious reasons. To get there we had to follow a dyke down to a wooden bridge, which we crossed to ascend the slope onto the pheasant land. A moorhen was spotted in the dyke but it dived into thick brambles and escaped. The pheasant land area is of interest to anyone who is keen on natural history. Abounding with bird and animal life, it is also blessed with numerous wild-flower species, such as the tall yellow spikes of Verbascum, or Greater Mullein and Evening Primrose, the beautiful blue and pink Vipers Bugloss and the unusual white Bladder Campion, to mention but a few.

When we had all assembled at the summit of the slope, we spread out in regular formation with the two dogs and their handlers out in front, followed by a line of short- and broad-winged hawks, while the rear was brought up by the falcons. It was agreed beforehand that no one should slip his hawk at quarry which did not break cover in his own line of flight, so avoiding a possible crabbing accident which could be caused by two over-enthusiastic falconers releasing their charges at one and the same quarry. A couple of young boys who were learning to become falconers were acting as beaters.

The formation temporarily broke up when a rabbit warren was discovered and we stood in readiness while the ferret was placed in a likely looking burrow. The Goshawks, Rudi included, were stationed on vantage points overlooking the warren ready to intercept any bunny which might bolt. But the tension soon relaxed as the familiar white face of the ferret appeared at the burrow nearest to my position, heralding the warren devoid of rabbits.

We regrouped just as a cock pheasant whirred away behind us, but it had gained too much of a head start and consequently, no hawks were slipped. Then a rabbit bolted from cover to the rear of Rudi and Wong-dai and made off for a huge thicket of brambles. The thicket was accordingly surrounded and we discovered that it concealed a huge rabbit warren. The ferret was removed from its travelling box again and went to ground for some considerable time. A rabbit showed its face at the entrance to one of the burrows and the tension mounted again. Then one of the young and inexperienced beaters glared down the hole and exclaimed in a loud voice that he could see two rabbits. Split seconds afterwards, no one could see any, for the rabbits had chosen to face the ferret rather than run the gauntlet above ground. Some 20 minutes later, the ferret resurfaced and we came to the conclusion that the rabbits must have dug themselves in. Rudi's talons gripped the glove convulsively as the ferret was placed back in its box for the second time.

We again regrouped and continued to beat the rough ground. I flushed a cock pheasant right in front of me and cast off Rudi after it. She was hard on its tail and both birds were flying as one, Rudi following every twist and turn of the pheasant. Finally, the pheasant became so hard-pressed that it dived into a patch of undergrowth that was choking a small bush. Rudi crashed in after it. I left the main body of the hawking party and found Rudi glaring angrily into the scrub. The pheasant was obviously still in there somewhere but it was not visible and the dogs were too far away to be called, so I had to be content with untangling Rudi's feathers from the thorns and set off to rejoin the group after giving her a small reward of meat for effort.

One of the beaters appeared on the brow of a hill to inform me that a rabbit had been marked down and as I turned to join him, the rabbit bolted in my direction. Rudi was soon off my fist but the rabbit evaded capture by diving beneath a wire fence. At the same instant, Slim's Bonelli's Eagle threw up over the fence whereupon he and Rudi almost collided in mid-air, but our troubles were by no means over, for both took stand in the same tree. They had been chasing the same rabbit from different angles and both Slim and I were unaware of each other's close proximity. Fortunately, both birds returned obediently to our respective fists.

Slim and I took up positions in the field directly below the pheasant rough, but keeping a respectful distance from each other while the remaining club members beat the shrubbery where the rabbit had put in. Another pheasant was flushed but it disappeared over the brow of the rough like greased lightning, followed by another rabbit which made the sanctuary of a gigantic warren. More than one ferret would have been required to work this one with any success, so we abandoned it and headed for another area of rough ground on the far side of the gravel ponds beyond the 'heron log', so called because this fallen tree trunk is a favourite perching place of wild herons.

Groups of Mallard, Tufted Duck, Pochard and a solitary Golden-eye left the smaller ponds as we passed them by but nothing presented itself for a decent slip for the hawks. Presently, we came upon a tall hawthorn hedge whereupon Slim, one of the dog handlers and myself worked one side while the remainder of the party worked the other. The going on our side was tough, with dying bindweed and goose-grass wrapping around our ankles causing us to stumble among the dead vegetation. No quarry was sighted and we had almost reached the end of our beat when a flurry of wings in the undergrowth caught the attention of Rudi's keen and ever alert eyes. She gripped the glove and craned her neck and I released my hold on her jesses, whereupon she plunged headlong into a bed of wilting nettles and briars. Out of the far side of the bed hurtled a cock pheasant which whirred away at almost the speed of sound. Rudi meanwhile became entangled in the briars and eventually poked her disappointed and frustrated face out of the gap where the pheasant had departed.

After that near miss, we all moved out on to the open marshy areas on the gravel beds to give our falcons a chance. A small party of beaters skirted the marshes to put up the waterfowl and when this was accomplished, the Lanner and a female Laggar Falcon were released. But they fared no better than the short-wings. The Laggar went up dangerously high and we all thought she was going on the soar, but she later came in to the lure. Both falcons appeared to be disinterested and after the Lanner was called in after a half-hearted stoop at a Mallard, an arm belonging to one of the dog handlers was noticed waving frantically in the air, heralding that a hare had been spotted lying in its form, but it had made good its escape by the time the Goshawks and eagle were in position.

Our hasty movements flushed a covey of partridges but the only fit falcon was not in a good enough position to risk a flight at them. We made our way back along the dyke in single file, myself in the lead, when a moorhen was flushed with Rudi hotly in pursuit. The moorhen splashed into the water and submerged, Rudi being defeated yet again. She threw up into a tree above the spot where the moorhen had put in and then began to act up by flying from one tree to another. After a few minutes of this appalling behaviour she flew down to my fist and I could tell from her actions that all these near misses were not going down too well from her point of view.

We pressed on and flushed a covey of six pheasants that came to rest on a cart-track which wended its dusty way across the centre of some sewage beds. The members of the party sat down to watch as I moved out across the beds to a position downwind of the pheasants and then began to walk them up, but unfortunately, they had all run into a very dense area of uncropped kale and ungathered sugar-beet and were not to be found. I had practically returned to the hawking party when a hen pheasant was flushed with Rudi only inches from its tail and in full pursuit; she really meant business. The flight was soon obscured by the undulating landscape of the pheasant land and I followed her as fast as the thorn scrub would allow.

Some time later, I heard her bells and located her beneath dense hawthorn shrubbery. She had lost the pheasant and came running out of the thicket to jump on to my fist. I gave her a small reward for superb effort and began to make my way back to the party when a rabbit jumped from a scant bramble patch in front of us, and for a moment I thought Rudi had saved the day and had succeeded in taking it, but alas, it had secured the safety of its burrow. Rudi was wedged into the hole up to her wing butts and I had to unceremoniously pull her out backwards. The hawking trip was concluded by a display of lure swinging and stooping by the falcons over the stubble.

Although nothing was caught on this occasion, we all considered we had enjoyed pounds' worth of excitement with thrilling flights occurring throughout the entire expedition. The one consolation, referred to earlier, was that the game missed this day was unharmed and would still be around to provide sport on future occasions. None of our game strayed far after being hawked at and could usually be found in more or less the same place on consecutive days. Although we failed to make a kill despite having in our possession some first-rate hawks, the day's sport was far from marred and everyone present enjoyed it to the full. In fact, it was even stated that the game had given us such a thrilling day that it would have been almost a pity if we *had* taken something.

It should also perhaps be pointed out that wild quarry, in its own natural habitat, is well aware of all the bolt-holes and escape routes and knows its area inside out, whereas the hawks are usually flying 'blind' as it were, rendering the quarry at least a 50–50 chance of escape.

Some weeks later, the same hawking party assembled for a field meeting on the Misk Hills in Hucknall, near Nottingham. It was a chilly November morning although the watery sun was doing its utmost to warm up the damp and pungent ground. The smell of wood-smoke was strong in our nostrils as it wafted on a gentle breeze from a farmer's fire further along the hills as he burned the remnants of the summer's hedge cuttings. The bracken was brown and dying off and the leaves were falling from the trees in their thousands. Soon the icy grip of winter would be upon the hills and hawking the high ground would become more difficult as the snow settled. We had gathered to have a last fling before winter enveloped everywhere with its white blanket of snow.

The previous day, Rudi had grabbed a Sheld duck belonging to a colleague. The duck had been grubbing about in a bed of dying nettles but was invisible to the naked eye; all I could see were the nettle stalks waving about and took the culprit to be either a rat or a rabbit. Consequently, Rudi was released. There came forth a tremendous uproar from the nettle beds and I spotted the flashing of white wings of a Sheld drake. Luckily, I managed to drag the irate Goshawk off the unfortunate duck, which had lost only a few feathers and its dignity, and release it. Rudi, however, was far from amused and was in a right royal temper at having been robbed of her prospective dinner. She stamped up and down on my fist with fury, so I promptly returned her to the mews with a morsel to pull at.

I was concerned that the incident might affect her flying on the Misk Hills, and my fears were justified. She bated away from me when I entered the mews in the early morning and would have nothing to do with me until we were on the hills and had been manned for an hour or so, then the sight of my ground-lure recaptured her attention for the job ahead. It was the general opinion that

we ought to try her at the lure first to ensure that she was going to be trust-
worthy, even though her weight was at the correct level and dropping. She
gripped the glove so sharply at the production of the lure that I abandoned my
original intention of flying her on a creance and let her go free in her own sweet
time as the lure was dragged across the hillside.

The very instant that she left the glove she ignored the lure completely and
flew off at a tangent, over the brow of the hill and into dense pine woods some
400 yards distant. I followed her into the wood and found her high up in a tall
pine, being mobbed without mercy by two magpies. At my approach she
sloped off and flew from one tree to another, leading me a merry dance in and
out of the wood. Eventually, she flew off high above the tops of the trees and
disappeared downwind. I searched alone for her all afternoon, combing every
wood for miles along the M1 motorway until finally, I tired of hearing
imaginary hawk bells and examining remarkably Goshawk-like stumps of tree
branches which continually played tricks with my eyes. My head was spinning
and my neck was aching with constant surveillance of the high trees, and, as
darkness set in, I had to abandon the search.

I never saw Rudi again. She had a good 40 square miles of immediate pine
forest in which to lose herself and equally large plantations abounded not far to
the north and west and the winds were directed well enough to drive her right
into them. Many years later, I discovered a Goshawks' eyrie in one of these
plantations and it is not unlikely that Rudi could have had something to do
with the formation of that eyrie. After all, it is largely due to escaped falconers'
birds that the Goshawk is now back with us as a British breeding species.

I paid a visit to my old friend Brian Ford at Burton on Trent and, during my
stay there, I met Bill Turner, a tall, bearded fellow with a great sense of
humour and who was destined to become a great friend. At that time, Bill lived
in Pelsall in Staffordshire and was flying an immature female Imperial Eagle
(*Aquila heliaca*), one of five imported by a Wolverhampton dealer. Bill
happened to mention that the dealer might consider selling an Imperial Eagle
to me, if I was so-minded. Eagles being my long standing favourites, I
considered the matter very deeply and I asked Bill to contact the dealer.

A week later, Bill rang to inform me that the dealer was considering parting
with one of the eagles and so the following morning, I drove down to Pelsall to
meet Bill, and from there we drove to Wolverhampton. The dealer showed us
his stock of birds on screen-perches, which comprised four Imperial Eagles in
immature plumage, which were in pristine condition apart from one hooded
bird with a swollen hind toe. I handled a fine example of one of the Imperials
while on the dealer's premises and was filled with desire to train and fly one of
these superb and rare birds. The dealer had agreed to a cash sale of £60 for the
bird that I had handled, which I considered to be the most attractive of the
four, not that that was a sound reason for choosing the bird, but she was
certainly the palest Imperial Eagle that I had seen.

Opposite page *I handled a fine example of an Imperial Eagle* (J. Eyett).

Above *Bill Turner with Ajax at a World Wildlife Fund event.*

Opposite page *Series of plumage changes during the past fourteen years of Ajax, the Imperial Eagle.* **Top left** *First year.* **Top right** *Third year.* **Below left** *Sixth year.* **Below right** *Fourteenth year.*

Imperial Eagles may take more than ten years before attaining their attractive dark chocolate-brown plumage, which, for some obscure reason, appears to be a longer period than for any other raptor, to my knowledge at least. Many other long-lived eagles lay only one egg every 18 months to 2 years. The post-fledgling period of this single youngster is a prolonged matter, requiring the combined efforts of both parents to raise it. Thus, it is just as well these eagles enjoy such longevity, for otherwise their species would soon become extinct through insufficient young to maintain the population. Compared with statistics such as these, the Imperial Eagle is quite prolific, two young being common-place and three not particularly rare, while there is at least one authentic case of an eyrie containing four eyasses. The notorious 'Cain and Abel' battle, where the eldest sibling very often kills the youngest chick, as in the Golden Eagle, does not occur so frequently, if at all, in the case of the Imperial Eagle. Therefore, most of the young hatched stand a good chance of fledging, so with such a potentially large fledgling population, the species ought to be more common than it is. Perhaps the long period of adolescence to maturity places the species in a vulnerable position, for the chances of a young Imperial reaching maturity without being shot, trapped or poisoned, must be rather slim. Size is also no criterion, as many eagles much larger in size than the Imperial attain adult plumage far in advance of the latter. Smaller eagles tend to fledge more rapidly anyway, but all I know for certain is that, as I write these lines, my Imperial Eagle is in her 14th year and still bears numerous light-coloured areas of immaturity.

My eagle was in her first year when I acquired her and was not unlike a very large Tawny Eagle in colouration, except that she was heavily streaked on the breast and her facial features differed markedly. She fed on the fist the first

evening in a darkened room, but before feeding her I placed her, hooded, on the scales where she tipped the 10 lb mark. I named her 'Ajax', after a Martial Eagle (*Polemaetus bellicosus*) of the same name from the book *Birds of the Gauntlet* by H. Von Michaelis, and she has since become a well-known eagle in falconry circles. She ranks high as one of the finest birds I have ever flown, not quite so majestic as Sable perhaps, but there has always been that certain something about Ajax.

I began the manning process almost immediately and found that, like Sable, Ajax too would bate at walls and fence-posts if they provided a pleasant-looking perching place. I also had to wash her primary and train (tail) feathers because

Above left *Ajax was in her first year when I acquired her.*

Above right *Not quite so majestic as Sable perhaps, but there has always been that certain something about Ajax.*

Below *I began the manning process immediately.*

they had become encrusted with mutes from the walls of the dealer's establishment. This was no simple task, for she was an extremely powerful bird and she
tried to slash me with her great beak every time I made a move. She had the
rather annoying habit of attempting to slash me in the face while manning her
and she still does this at odd times to this very day. She is trained but not tamed,
her spirit remains unbroken, and yet at the same time, she shows a high degree
of affection for me to the exclusion of everyone else.

This seems rather contrary, for after her attempts to slash me in the face or
stab me with a set of her great black talons, just how can one speak of
affection? I firmly believe that she does not try to attack me in the true sense of
the word, but rather that I am the sole food provider and the only way that she
can take food from me is with her heavy armour. Should I be tardy in
producing her eagerly awaited meal, she is likely to speed up the proceedings
somewhat by grabbing me, or at least, attempting to, for I have learned over
the years to anticipate this kind of behaviour and usually place the target area
well out of reach split seconds beforehand. At such times, she probably regards
me as the prey animal, so to speak.

One week later, Ajax was flying free to the fist and ground-lure and it was
also time for her Fowl-pest injection, the first of two which were organised by
the Leicestershire Falconer's Club. The disease had been sweeping the country
in epidemic proportions and such immunisation projects were becoming
commonplace. I held Ajax bodily while the vet injected intramuscularly four
cc's of the dead vaccine 'Newcadin'. There were no after- or side-effects and
most of the club hawks were subsequently vaccinated.

I joined Bill Turner for a weekend's hawking in Staffordshire. As always
when I visit Bill, bedtime was ignored and most of the night was spent talking
hawks, this particular occasion being no exception. In fact, it was worse, for in
the small hours, Bill jumped up from his comfortable armchair, relit the
cinders in his pipe-bowl and insisted that we walk the eagles around the village
of Pelsall to clear the cobwebs from our sleepy minds. We finally returned at
4 am in the morning after numerous glances from the police in passing patrol
cars.

Bill's Imperial had developed a large growth on its lores, between the eye
and cere, stretching the lores to their maximum. I suggested that we first
contact a vet, for it resembled a tumour or a cyst, and after flying both the
eagles the following morning, we telephoned a local vet and visited the surgery
in the evening where I restrained the eagle while the vet pushed a hypodermic
needle into the centre of the swelling and inserted some antibiotic ointment into
the hole, obviously assuming that it was some sort of infection. In short, the vet
was at a loss as to what it was or what could be done, but on the way home I
told Bill that, in my limited opinion, it was nothing more than a cyst, and if so,
it could probably be excised. Bill drove slowly, obviously giving the matter
some thought, then put his foot down sharply on the accelerator and said that if
I was prepared to risk the operation, then so was he.

On arrival at his home, Bill held the eagle while his wife, Tricia, held the
bird's head still so that I could begin the task. Swabbing the lump and

A study of the third eyelid, or nictitating membrane of Ajax. **Above right** *Membrane not visible.* **Above** *Partly visible.* **Left** *Totally exposed. This membrane is used to protect the eye surface.*

surrounding tissue with surgical spirit, I then used a sterilised razor blade to cut a cross in the swelling. Seconds later, the entire inside of the swelling fell out onto the carpet, a definite cyst. It resembled a conker with its spiked kernel intact. The gaping hole was clean with no bits of the cyst remaining, so I packed it with sulphonamide as a precaution against harmful bacteria entering and causing an infection. The wound healed without a scar.

Chapter 10

Falconry in the family

Jill, my wife-to-be, had planned our wedding date to fall upon my birthday, Midsummer's Day, and instead of the usual wedding bells, we thought it would be more appropriate, cheaper too, to walk down the aisle to the sound of hawk bells. The two page boys were to carry hooded falcons and falconer guests were also encouraged to bring a hawk along.

On the eve of our wedding, Bill and Tricia Turner, who had since moved from Staffordshire to a Forestry Commission posting near Hawick in Roxburgh, south-east Scotland, arrived bringing with them their Wallace's Hawk Eagle (*Spizaetus nanus*). Along with other colleagues I enjoyed a falconer's stag night which ended during the small hours. Most of the conversation that night was centred on hawking rather than marital bliss, so much so, that we almost forgot the purpose of our being there! The next morning I was a bundle of nerves, as I suppose most prospective husbands are, if they are honest. The page boys looked smart in their Scottish attire of kilt, sporrans and the like and both carried hooded Laggar Falcons, possibly the first falcons to attend a Nottinghamshire wedding for hundreds of years.

We arrived at St Matthias' church near my old home town of Carlton where I joined my brother at the altar as he was officiating as best man. The tinkling of hawk bells and the striking up of the organ informed me that my bride had arrived. From then on, the nerve-wracking ceremony was like any other marriage service, except for the intermittent bell-ringing as one falcon or another scratched its head with its foot.

At a field meeting I organised with a few colleagues on the Misk Hills a few weeks later, very few hawks were flown owing to exceptionally high winds. Ajax was one of the few who were flown and her performance was thrilling. The wind took her up high as she was cast off the ridge and when she had attained a height of 100 feet or so, she plunged down vertically at me in a series of savage stoops which I have yet to see bettered by any falcon. Twice she hit me at full tilt and once sent me sprawling in the grass. She was in the peak of flying condition and I held high hopes of a fruitful hawking session in Scotland when we departed for Bill Turner's home a few days later.

We took Ajax onto the wild, rugged Scottish hills to search for rabbits. We carried her onto the tops of the slopes, high above a steep-sided valley, which

Above left *Wedding-day, with hooded falcons in attendance.*
Left *Jill, my wife, with a male Red Tailed Hawk.*
Above *The winds took her up high as she was cast off the ridge* (F. Bradley).

was cloaked with large patches of purple heather and blaeberries. A shallow burn wended its way in the valley below, although it only looked like a pencil line from our vantage point. A few rabbits were out on the slopes with Ajax putting in some thrilling downwind stoops, missing by mere fractions, then pulling out and levelling off to soar out over the valley, before returning to my gauntlet. Ajax used the thermals and updraughts to her advantage and her overall flying was far superior in the hill country to that of the lowlands. How I wished I had ready access to such immense slopes in my own area.

The lush vegetation on the banks of the burn was a strong contrast to that of the sheep-cropped hills. In the marshy areas, the insectivorous Round-leaved Sundew and star-shaped leaves and purple flowers of the Butterwort grew on the thick carpet of saturated sphagnum moss. Fragrant and Heath-Spotted Orchids thrust up their pink flower spikes alongside the yellow, ball-shaped flower heads of the Globe Flower. Moving rapidly through the cover was a large covey of Black Grouse, which exploded from hiding and whirred away downwind, covering a good mile or so before putting in to a patch of heather.

As usual, Bill and I chatted far into the night, long after everyone else had retired to bed. To keep ourselves awake we went for a walk down by the burn, where I was rather surprised to find out just how dark the night can be without the glare of street lamps for miles around. We were literally groping about in the dark and almost ended up in the burn with the trout and salmon on numerous occasions. We found a huge pine log which I considered would make a suitable perch for Ajax, so we shouldered it between us and carried it over the moor and through the deer forest back home. I took the log back to England with me where, even today, it is still Ajax's favourite perch.

All too soon our short holiday came to a close and we had to return to the grimy Midlands. The air in Scotland had seemed so clean and pure that I detested every mile of our southward journey. My idea of paradise would be to live in a crofter's cottage somewhere in the more remote parts of the Highlands of Scotland and I really envy the stalkers and gamekeepers who spend their days on those glorious hills.

It was about this time that Jill and I moved into our new house. For many months we had been living with my parents and this was the first time that I had ever left home. The new house was in need of decoration and the garage had to undergo major repairs to its roof before it could be converted into a mews fit for eagles. To complicate matters, Jill had to go into hospital for the birth of our first child, Joanne, so, needless to say, the hawks had to take a back seat for a few weeks, although I did manage to produce and circulate the first magazine for the East Midlands Hawking Club.

After Jill's convalescence, I was able to return to my hawks and re-enseamed Ajax ready to take the field. Two rabbits had succumbed to her murderous talons when one day Jill noticed that she had been lying down on the grass for much of the morning. I had put her out to weather in the early morning sunshine before going off to work and she was fine then, but when I returned at lunchtime it was evident that all was not well with her. I brought her indoors but she was unable to stand. Her left leg appeared to be causing her great pain and she could not bear her weight on it. Finally, she vomited a stream of foul-smelling liquid. Fearing that her leg was broken, I telephoned a local vet to arrange for an X-ray and managed to get her in immediately. Upon seeing the eagle, the vet was naturally apprehensive about handling her, so I had to do the job. While I stretched out Ajax's leg under the radiography machine, I must have accidentally put her leg back into joint again, for when we let her up, she could walk and grip as normal. Fortunately, she had somehow dislocated and not broken it.

Later that year, we migrated north again to visit Bill Turner for a few days. He had moved from Craik Forest and was now employed as a gamekeeper on Lord Rothewick's Scottish estate at Darvel in Ayrshire on the west coast. Bill's cottage was perched on the summit of a hill and entirely surrounded by grouse moors with a hugh deer forest in the valley to the rear of the cottage. Most of the deer were Roe with a few Japanese Sika here and there. Both breeds were very shy and the best chance of seeing either of them was in the early morning or towards dusk. It was while we were at Bill's that I learned of the death of

Above *Ajax sitting on her favourite perch, the pine log from Scotland.*

Right *Ajax takes a breath of fresh air during a break in our journey through Scotland.*

Walter Joynson, the highly esteemed and colourful Scottish falconer with whom I had corresponded recently on a regular basis. He had passed away some three weeks prior to my visit and I had planned to join him at his home at Kinlochard in Stirling during my stay. Falconry had lost one of its most loyal supporters and the news of his demise stunned me.

On a clear day the Isle of Arran was plainly visible from Bill's door-step as a solid black rock set in a glistening sea some 20 miles to the west. We had a closer view of Arran when we went down to the coast to Ayr for the day. The sea was cold but crystal clear and as I looked out across the waves I had a forlorn hope that I would catch a glimpse of one of Arran's Golden Eagles, which, Bill had informed me, often hunted his beat on the mainland. But I was not that fortunate and had to be content with Greater Black Backed Gulls.

Later that evening, Bill took me out into the wooded hills near his home. This area is known as Changue Forest and within minutes of entering this vast deer forest I saw two Sparrowhawks. Although breathtakingly beautiful, there was also an aura of mystery and something sinister about this primeval forest and I couldn't help thinking about how many unfortunate Jacobite clansmen must have hidden from the English redcoats in its dark, dank recesses. We followed a deer trail out of the forest onto the fringes of the grouse moor. Rabbits and Blue Hares were all over the place and we decided to fly Ajax at them in the morning.

Ajax was carried hooded to the tops of the grouse moor.

Ajax prepared for flight

The next day the moor was shrouded in a thick, clinging mist, which allowed us to position ourselves on the high tops without being observed by the intended quarry. By that time the sun was out and the mist receded rapidly. I handed Ajax over to Bill so that he could have a flight with her while I moved forward to beat a few rabbits out of the heather. I heard Bill shout and the next instant Ajax was off, but not at the intended rabbit, she was instead, making a powered dive at me. I tried to get out of her way, only to feel the full force of her paralysing talons squeezing the life out of my buttocks. I perambulated all over the heather-clad hillside with an infuriated Imperial Eagle hanging onto my backside, simply refusing to let go. Bill was rolling with mirth, but eventually he came up to relieve me. My eyes were streaming with pain from the wounds in my gored rear-end. Ajax had seen a piece of rabbit fur which I had carelessly left sticking out of my hawking bag and she had made a bee-line for it, only I spoilt her chances by swinging around and placing my cheeks in her flight path. She had not deliberately attacked me, for she soon released her hold, much to my relief. It had certainly made Bill's day.

Within minutes, she was on the wing again after a Blue Hare, which she chased over the skyline and out of sight. We followed in her wake just in time to observe her tearing a lapwing in half and swallowing the first portion whole.

The remainder of the lapwing disappeared into her crop as I took her up and, as that was more than enough to take the edge off her appetite, it concluded the day's hawking. The lapwing was an entirely unintentional quarry from my point of view, for I would much rather have seen her take the hare, but even so I think it unlikely that many falconers have taken a lapwing with a trained eagle, for the lapwing is an unbelievably manoeuvrable bird. The actual kill was obscured by the brow of the hill, so we will never know for certain whether she took it in fair flight or surprised it on the ground.

The remainder of the day was spent searching on the moors for plant specimens to take home to my father. Insectivorous Sundews and Butterworts were again much in evidence along the marshy areas of the burns and Heath-Spotted, Fragrant and Lesser-Butterfly Orchids dotted the slopes of the moors. Green-flowered Twayblade Orchids grew around the edges of the deer forest along with the beautiful golden orbs of the Globe Flower and delicate pink petals of Ragged Robin. We regretfully had to leave Ayrshire the following morning though even earlier than planned, as mist enveloped the moors and threatened to blot out our homeward journey. Luckily, we cleared the high country before the mist caught us and we made the long, uneventful trail safely back home.

Ajax's performance is always so much the better for a trip to Scotland and I also believe that she gets a bit above herself from such airings. For instance, on our return from this Scottish trip, she became decidedly aggressive for the first few days and I had to be very wary when she was on the loose, for on one occasion she flew round me in a tight circle and then hit me from behind. I was wearing casual summer clothing at the time and the result was a torn and ruined shirt plus two lacerations to my back. As I said before, the only specific reason I can give for this behaviour is that she possibly considered I was too tardy in rewarding her. Certainly, the only way she knows how to obtain her food is by the use of beak or talon, usually both, consequently, any unguarded part of my person blocking her path was sure to become a target.

Often have I read of a popular theory that eagles use only their feet as weapons and do not strike with their beaks. I venture to dismiss that theory as utter nonsense, as all of my eagles, Ajax in particular, will use her beak immediately on anyone, including myself, who dares to stroke her. To me, she is trained but not tamed and there is a vast difference between the two. She has lost nothing of her wild spirit and I love her for it. Not for me the docile, domesticated shadow of the true eagle that is sometimes the captive eagle in the wrong hands. I am sure the true eagle-lover will understand exactly what I mean.

In the autumn of 1973, Mr John Swift, then manager of the Trust House Forte hotel, the Angel and Royal at Grantham in Lincolnshire, telephoned me to ask if I would consider bringing Ajax along to appear in a mediaeval banquet at the hotel. Little did I realise at the time that these banquets were to play a large part in my future life and were to continue for many years virtually every Friday night during the winter months. However, before appearing at the banquet I, together with the East Midlands Hawking Club, attended a

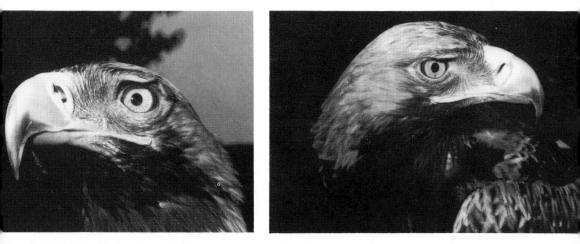

Above left *Ajax will use her beak immediately on anyone who dares to stroke her.*
Above right *Ajax has lost nothing of her wild spirit.*

meeting of falconers held in the grounds of Harewood House, just north of Leeds in Yorkshire. The meeting, to discuss impending legislation, was to coincide with a flying demonstration for the general public and was organised between Mr Peter Brown, then curator of the splendid bird garden at Harewood, and the Northern England Falconer's Club. Only at the annual Game Fair had I seen a gathering of so many falconers and only at falconry centres had I seen so many hawks on one weathering ground.

A large marquee was provided, with numerous photographs and articles of falconry furniture on display, providing an educational backdrop in addition to the weathering hawks. Two flying demonstrations were staged for the afternoon, the first one being composed entirely of falcons. For the second demonstration Peter Brown had approached me with a view towards flying Ajax from the roof of Harewood House, the stately home of the Earl and Countess of Harewood and home of that famous falconer of the past, the Hon Gerald Lascelles. I had never done anything of this magnitude with Ajax before. Flying her from the tops of deserted and remote grouse moors was one thing, this was entirely another. What the outcome would be I could only speculate, however, so anxiously keeping fingers crossed I entered the arena while one of our falconers, together with Peter Brown, took Ajax through the stately home and out on to the roof. I could barely see Ajax, but had given instructions that she be unhooded as soon as a suitable vantage point for the flight had been reached, so that she had time to take stock of the situation. A falcon had been flying while preparations for this epic flight were under way, but it had been brought in to the lure and I was standing alone in the arena. A deathly hush came over the large crowd encircling me. Gripping the whistle between my teeth, I emitted two shrill blasts, but for a second nothing happened. Then I saw Ajax spread her immense wings and launch into the sky. With hardly a wing-beat, she sailed the whole distance, floating above the heads of the astounded

Above left *Ajax flew from the roof of Harewood House above the heads of the aghast crowd . . .* (J. Kershaw Studios, York).

Left *. . . to alight perfectly on my fist in the centre of the arena* (J. Kershaw Studios, York).

Above *As we left the arena, the cameras began flashing by the dozen* (J. Kershaw Studios, York).

crowd to alight perfectly on my fist in the centre of the arena.

The crowd were numbed with awe and amazement and, be it known, so was I; deservedly Ajax received quite an ovation. As I left the arena for another hawk to be put on the wing, the cameras began flashing by the dozen, photographers everywhere were eager to obtain an image of the magnificent bird perched upon my fist. For our efforts, we were awarded a hawking trip on the Harewood estates and the display we gave became an annual event while Peter Brown was curator.

Then came the evening for my debut at the mediaeval banquet, held at the Angel and Royal Hotel in Grantham. The hotel, which is situated on the main road through Grantham, is reputed to be the oldest known hotel in Europe and has been known to travellers on the Great North Road for hundreds of years. In the King's Room, where the banquet was to be held, King Richard III in 1483 wrote in his own hand a letter to the Lord Chancellor bidding him send the Great Seal so that he might proclaim the treachery of his cousin, the second Duke of Buckingham. In the main bar, an original 14th century fireplace was discovered in 1947, while the walls were being stripped for decoration. This has

Left *Ajax on my fist after the Harewood display* (J. Kershaw Studios, York).
Above *Ajax and myself at a mediaeval display.*
Below *Philip Astle and Paul Williamson, with Ajax and myself at the Angel and Royal Hotel mediaeval banquet* (A. Reynolds Photographics, Grantham, Lincs).

now been restored to use, and in recent years more than one deer and swine carcase has been roasted over the embers. King John was lodged at the Angel and Royal in 1213, but its title commemorates a specific royal visit, that of the Prince of Wales (later Edward VII) in 1866.

Thus steeped in history, I ventured into this famous building one rainy Friday evening with Ajax upon my fist and bedecked in colourful mediaeval attire, hand-made for the occasion by Jill. There I met Mike Houghton, an archer of international repute, a great friend and a great character with whom I was to perform at mediaeval banquets for many years. His partner in those early days was Nigel Bampton who used a crossbow with devastating effect. In addition to Mike and Nigel, who were dressed as a Saxon yeoman and Knight of the Realm respectively, there was Alan Snowden, a superb court jester, plus a band of minstrels and a bevy of delightful serving wenches.

At the beginning of each banquet a 'King and Queen' are selected from the guests, together with another couple who also sat at the King's table as the Sheriff and his Lady. After a glass or two of mead, or some other such sweet wine, taken in the foyer, the guests are ushered into the King's Room led by the King himself and escorted by the knights and court jester. The meal begun, the jester, minstrels and serving wenches play out their respective roles while the knights stroll around the room, broadswords drawn and looking very dignified. I personally do not normally arrive until after the meal is well under way when, on a fanfare from the minstrels and a verbal introduction by the jester, I enter the room as the Royal Court Falconer, holding Ajax aloft as a preview of the 'cabaret' to come. Ajax is also kept hooded throughout the evening, except of course, for the flight at the finale.

After the banquet and a mock battle by the knights I make an appearance with Ajax. The guests are treated to a short briefing on falconry in mediaeval times and then Ajax is unhooded and placed on a chair-back at one end of the roof while I venture to the opposite end and call her to the fist, allowing the vast majority of the guests their first glimpse of an eagle in 'free-flight'. She is flown totally free and her wing-tips are only inches away from the merry faces of the guests. After three or four flights of this nature, Ajax is rehooded and I leave the aisle to Mike and Nigel who prepare for an archery tournament.

*   *   *

At about this period in time, a colleague was going into the Formula One racing car business and would no longer have the time to fly his Steppe Eagle. He telephoned me one evening with the result that I made an excursion to his home in Staffordshire to buy the immature female eagle for £60. One of my main reasons for purchasing the bird was a desire to fly it as a cast with Ajax. Only on extremely rare occasions have eagles been flown in casts, especially where different species are concerned. The only exponent in recent years to my knowledge was the late Captain Charles Knight (uncle of Phillip Glasier) who flew Crowned, Martial and Golden Eagles in the air simultaneously.

The Steppe Eagle, which I named 'Ares', had to undergo foot surgery before any use could be made of her. Both hind toes were severely infected and it was almost a month before she could be put on the wing. Although she was not much smaller than Ajax, her temperament was entirely different. She was as gentle as Ajax was savage. Her flying was a pleasure to behold, frequently soaring in great circles to land like a butterfly upon my gauntlet, with none of the insane crashing assaults of Ajax. On numerous occasions she stayed aloft in strong lift areas for several minutes, coming down only when called. She was exhilarated by the joys of flying.

Ajax and Ares flew superbly as a cast with none of the expected aggression from the former. In fact at one stage, Ajax alighted on the top of a telegraph pole and Ares landed upon her back, where she remained for a few moments before launching off into space again to choose a more stable vantage point. Cast flying the two eagles became one of the highlights of my falconry career, but one morning, tragedy struck when I discovered that Ares had mysteriously broken her right leg. An X-ray was arranged in consultation with a local vet and within hours it was cast in a plastic tube with a foam rubber lining on the inside to prevent chafing. The casing was a success, and after three weeks it was removed and Ares was reclaimed to take the field.

The vet was of the opinion that she was deficient in calcium, and events backed up his theory when some weeks later, she broke her left leg. Never before in my life had any of my birds suffered from broken bones, yet this poor eagle had sustained two compound fractures in a matter of weeks. Her equipment was examined and re-examined for faults of some nature, but none were evident. Finally, I had to accept the vet's theory that Ares was 'brittle-boned' and was fed accordingly with a liquid calcium supplement administered in her food.

That winter I designed two permanent perches for the eagles to use at night and during spells of inclement weather. A trip to the local scrapyard was necessary to obtain 12 old car tyres, six for each perch. The tyres were laid one on top of the other to form a type of barrel, then a metal rod with a loop at the top was placed in the centre of the tyres, which were then filled to the brim with concrete. Almost a week passed before the concrete dried sufficiently to tether

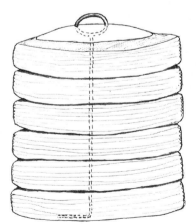

Tyre-perch. Designed especially for eagles by David Fox.

Left *Myself with the female from my pair of European Eagle Owls which failed to breed.*

Below left *The male Eagle Owl.*

Right *My imprinted male Kestrel refused all advances from females of its own kind.*

the eagles by their leashes to the loops, but once finished, they proved to be revolutionary. I abolished the screen-perch afterwards, for these new perches were far superior in that should the birds become ill, they could lie down on the concrete 'ledge' instead of hanging upside down from the screen and wasting valuable energy in trying to regain it. Also, the concrete itself, resembling natural stone, kept their talons a respectable length without the need for coping. The perches were easily regained after a bate and in no way could any eagle, or a Hereford bull for that matter, pull one over, for they each weighed over two tons.

Ever since the breeding attempt with Orion and Medusa I had been longing to reproduce, in captivity, young from various species of birds of prey. Mostly, through lack of knowledge, my attempts failed miserably. A pair of Eagle Owls that I tried for four years dug so many nest scrapes that I thought they were either going to breed at any moment, or else dig their way out of the aviary. Unfortunately, not one egg, fertile or otherwise, was ever produced by this pair. I attempted no fewer than five separate pairings using different females with an imprinted male Kestrel, but he was so imprinted to the human form, having been hand-reared from a small chick, that he attacked all five out of sheer malice, almost blinding one and nearly killing two others. He probably would have completed the job too had I not intervened and parted them. Yet

My pair of arctic Snowy Owls in their skylight-seclusion aviary.

he certainly had been in breeding condition, for he had displayed sexually towards me every time I entered the aviary.

Successes at Cornell University in America drifted back to a small group of us in our area who were interersted in raptor breeding and we began to benefit from their discoveries. To begin with, I scrapped the open-plan wire-mesh type aviaries that I had used in the past, erecting in their place, the new so-called skylight and seclusion type. In my case, these were merely large wooden pens with open plan mesh roofs. Six inches or so beneath the wire mesh I fitted a layer of nylon garden netting, the type used to keep sparrows away from the strawberries. Trapdoors were built into the sides to allow the baths to be filled and cleaned, the food to be deposited and any other necessary chore to be performed without the necessity of having to enter the aviary one self, so eliminating the possibility of unduly disturbing the nervous inmates. Although certain hawks have been bred in the conventional open-mesh type of aviary, I believe the skylight seclusion design is far superior, basically because the occupants cannot see out and therefore are not disturbed by visual upsets. Because of the open top, the vegetation grows naturally and waste food, should there be any, will decompose rapidly in the normal manner with the help of insects and the elements. An almost natural environment can be created.

I obtained many papers and kept a file of captive breeding techniques, which included the use of artificial insemination, various types of incubator, egg-pulling and double-clutching to increase output. It all seemed very technical to begin with, but year by year, I unravelled a little more of the tangle, until today, my raptor-breeding colleagues and I have a clearer understanding of the principles involved. Nowadays, we are producing our own birds for the sport of falconry, for the continuance of further breeding projects, to further knowledge and, ultimately, for the release of captive-produced examples to augment endangered wild stocks.

I worked closely with several colleagues and, during the early years, we experimented mainly with Kestrels. One of my colleagues had set up an aviary for our joint pair of Kestrels. We learned a lot from that pair which we designated as a test-bed for our future 'experiments'. They provided us with many answers and caused me to become deeply involved in artificial incubation techniques. All my research came to fruition in 1981, although on account of a spot of outside interference, the whole programme almost ended before it had begun. The birds in question were a pair of Sparrowhawks. I had particularly wanted to breed the Sparrowhawk in captivity for a variety of reasons. First, they are the most suitable hawks for flying over the local terrain, which is inhabited by a super-abundance of natural quarry. Secondly, if lost while flying, there would be no problems relating to the 'release' of foreign birds, for the Sparrowhawk is a relatively common British species. Thirdly, the Sparrowhawk is notoriously difficult to train and keep in flying order, and, as such, is possibly just as difficult to breed from, therefore it offered me a challenge. I believed that if I could breed the Sparrowhawk in captivity, then other species should not prove too difficult in the future. I hoped.

The 1981 season was my third with this particular pair of hawks. They had hit it off from the very beginning, laying their first clutch of beautifully marked eggs in their first year with me. However, despite the fact that I had placed a couple of suitable nesting sites in the aviary, the female chose to lay her first clutch on the ground beneath an elderberry bush. At a colleague's suggestion, I pulled the eggs from her one by one, transferring them to his Hova-bactor incubator. Egg-pulling however, is more successful when each egg is taken shortly after laying, but in my case, still being a little 'green', I always left her with one egg, taking the oldest egg on each visit. A breeder in America has apparently obtained a total of 23 eggs from his Coopers Hawk in this manner, most of which were fertile. However, hatching dates came and went and none of my total of six eggs showed any signs of pipping. Consequently, my colleague had them blown, when one of them was found to contain a partially formed, but very dead chick. This at least was encouraging, for it showed that copulation had taken place.

The following season she laid another six eggs in a nesting tray which I had fixed onto the aviary wall. In this tray I had previously deposited an abundance of nesting material, but unfortunately, she threw most of it out and layed her eggs on the bare wooden floor of the tray. I hadn't realised this until it was too late. Consequently, the eggs rolled about all over the place and some received more incubation than others. Once incubation has begun, no eggs can withstand such partial brooding, the heat must be maintained for the embryo to survive. By the time I discovered the dilemma, it was too late to do anything

about it. Although I had failed, primarily through my own carelessness, the theory was rammed home to my addled brain that the deep cup-shaped lining was the all-important factor in keeping the eggs all in one place, directly under the female. That winter, I resolved that if I failed in 1981 it would not be for stupid reasons of that nature. I had already planned to double-clutch, that is to say, to remove the first clutch so that she could recycle and lay a repeat, that way, I could have two bites of the cherry, so to speak. But in order to carry out such a project, I needed a suitable incubator.

Now there are many incubators of various descriptions on the market, but usually they follow two basic types: the still-air, which is often of the manual-turning type, and the forced-draught automatic turner. Eggs have to be turned a number of times daily to relieve pressure at the point where the egg is resting, rather like ourselves when we have been sitting in one position for a while and suddenly feel the need to shift to a more comfortable position to allow the blood to begin flowing again through the compressed portion. Turning also prevents the egg-shell membranes from sticking to the sides and retains the yolk in the centre of the egg, allowing ease of hatching at pipping time.

Both types of incubator are suitable for the hatching of hawk eggs, but I

Left *The male, or musket, from my breeding pair of Sparrowhawks.*
Below left *The female from my breeding pair of Sparrowhawks.*
Below *The Turn-X6A automatic turning, forced-draught incubator. Turner on right and water fountain on left.*

Sparrowhawk eggs in turning grid, dome of Turn-X removed.

decided to go for the forced-draught, automatic-turning variety, on account of the fact that if I desired a day out sometime during the month of incubation, I could do so without fear of affecting the precious eggs. Having decided upon the type of incubator I required, the next problem was selecting the model. My output of eggs per annum was obviously only going to be small, so a small portable incubator was all that I needed.

Fortunately, a colleague, Mr Robin Haigh, had gone into business of marketing falconry equipment, including incubators, and he was not only able to supply me with much valuable information, but also sent me an American Marsh Farms Turn-X6A automatic-turning, forced-draught incubator. The incubator was set to run at one hundred degrees, but there was a thermostat regulator fitted, enabling me to reduce the temperature to 99° Fahrenheit, dropping to 98° at minimum. These latter temperatures appear more suitable to the successful hatching of hawk eggs.

Having obtained the incubator, I was all set and raring to go, but it was only late January and the earliest the hawks had laid was early May, although the breeding season had begun for the pair were continually calling to each other. Everything seemed to be running smoothly until that fateful morning of February 3. I was doing my rounds of the aviaries, feeding the occupants in turn until I came to the Sparrowhawk's aviary. I lifted the food-hatch to deposit the day's quota of food when I noticed that the meat I had placed in the previous morning lay untouched on the food-hatch. This was most unusual, for even if they did not eat it outright, they usually cached it somewhere. Either way, it was seldom left on the food hatch.

Everything was in order on the outside of the aviary, it was still padlocked and there was no sign of forced entry that I could see. At the side of the aviary was a dead apple tree which I often used as an observation post if I needed to view the complete interior of the pen and this I scaled as rapidly as possible. With my heart in my mouth, I peered over the lip of the aviary but, to my horror, no signs of life were visible. My first thoughts were that a rat or some other four-footed predator had got into the pen and killed the pair, or perhaps a hole had appeared somewhere. Of one thing I was certain, the Sparrowhawks had vanished into thin air, but after a whole hour of scrupulous inspection, not one hole could be detected and no piles of Sparrowhawk feathers littered the floor of the aviary. So what was amiss? The only item left to check was the padlock itself, whereupon I discovered that all that was required to open it was a piece of bent wire or the blade of a knife. So, it was theft! My first feelings were of sickness, then bitter disappointment and finally, rage. Had I been able to lay my hands on the thief I would not have been responsible for my actions. All my plans for the forthcoming breeding season now lay in ruin.

My immediate reaction was to telephone the local police station at Beeston who sent round an officer to investigate the crime. We found the tell-tale boot-marks in the soil of our neighbour's garden and the point at which they came over the fence. The officer shared my fears that the hawks had been stolen, but he added that he thought juveniles might be the culprits, suggesting that I ought to inform the local news media to warn parents, should their children suddenly 'acquire' a pair of valuable hawks. I did as he suggested and contacted the *Nottingham Evening Post* who published an article the following evening.

If theft was going to be a major threat in the future, I decided that now would be as good a time as any to guard against it, so much of the following Saturday was spent studying various burglar alarm systems and purchasing a number of heavy duty padlocks. Jill and I arrived home rather late that same evening, but we had only been in a few moments when the telephone rang. I was busy doing something so Jill answered it. Looking up from my task, I caught the blank expression on Jill's face as she placed the receiver back on the hook. For some agonising seconds, I could get nothing out of her, so shocked was she. Just when I was beginning to think that someone near and dear to us had passed away, she gave me the message from the caller. It was short, sharp and straight to the point: 'Tell Mr Fox his Sparrowhawks are back in the aviary!'

I was through the back door and out into the garden in seconds. Before I even began to look through the spy-holes of the aviary, I knew that someone had been present in our absence, for the aviary door which I had left ajar, was now closed, secured by a piece of pine-wood inserted into the hasp and staple. Despite the gathering gloom, both hawks could be seen side by side on one of the perches. It was like the answer to a prayer, a miracle.

The piece of pine-wood was immediately replaced with one of the heavy-duty padlocks and then I informed the police of the situation. That night, Jill and I talked at some length, trying to unravel the mystery. We could under-stand the motives for taking the hawks in the first place, but to risk being caught by bringing them back seemed illogical to me. It would have been far simpler to have released them, or even killed them and buried the bodies to hide the evidence. Although in no way could I forgive the thieves for breaking in and taking the hawks, I was grateful for their prompt return.

My main worry now, apart from further thefts, was the nagging question of whether the disturbance had damaged permanently the courtship cycle, which had just begun prior to their theft. Only time would tell. Their feathers were bent and soiled, indicating that they had probably been kept in a confined space. The female had been wearing her Aylmeri bracelets, for she had been flown in falconry in her first season. I had purposely left them on in the possible event that she might attempt to kill the male, or musket, as is sometimes the case when a pair of Sparrowhawks are placed together. With the bracelets left on the female, it would simply be a matter of threading the jesses through the eyelets and removing her from the pen. I know of several cases where the un-timely execution of the musket by the female has abruptly terminated the breeding attempt. Luckily, no conflict was ever observed with this particular pair, in fact quite the contrary, they were quite a pair of 'love-birds' from the outset. Even so, I took the precaution of leaving ample food on the food-hatch that night, for I had no way of knowing when they had last fed and I had no desire for the musket to become the female's first meal.

The following morning I rose early to check the hawks, especially the Sparrowhawks. They were difficult to spot amongst the shrubbery, but I

Aylmeri jesses showing bracelets on a Prairie Falcon.

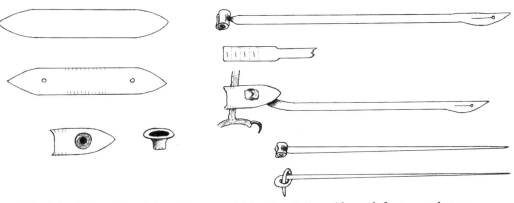

The Aylmeri Jess. Named after its inventor, Major Guy Aylmer. **Above left, top to bottom:** *Bracelet pattern; bracelet prepared; bracelet complete with eyelet; eyelet.* **Above right, top to bottom:** *Mews jess (button type); method of preparing button; Aylmeri jess complete; Aylmeri field jesses.*

eventually detected the musket feeding on the aviary floor then the female suddenly flew off the food-hatch with a piece of meat in her talons. She flew a couple of circuits around the aviary until she dropped the portion of food, whereupon she took stand on her favourite perch. Both birds were obviously more nervous than usual and it was clear that the theft was having its effects.

However, towards the end of April, there was much activity and uttering of peculiar twittering calls from the pair. In previous years they had laid their first egg on May 6 and 12 respectively, although in both cases, laying had been preceded by harsh hecking calls, this twittering was a new one on me and I began to wonder if it was the musket calling in fear of the female. Again, only time and careful observation would tell. The female was particularly restless, flying from perch to perch. Three days later, the harsh, falcon-like call returned and I felt a little more relieved. Perhaps breeding would take place after all. As soon as I peered through the spy-holes, the female attacked me, her long yellow toes protruding through the hole. In future I would have to be more careful, for one could very easily lose an eye after such an assault.

As the days went by, the calling grew more intense and the attacks on the spy-holes where I was observing increased in ferocity. For the first time since the theft, I now believed I was in with a chance.

During the first days of May, the female spent much of her time on low perches, she seemed heavy with eggs, but perhaps that was wishful thinking on my part. On May 8, she laid her first egg in one of the pine and wire-mesh nests I had constructed and fitted into the elderberry tree. I was absolutely delighted. All that remained now was for the eggs to be fertile and to raise the young! As was usual with the female of this pair, she laid a total of six eggs, the first on May 8 and the other five on May 10, May 13, May 15, May 18 and May 20. The nest I had constructed remained unaltered except for a lining of fine twigs.

The weather was colder than usual for the time of year, with much rain,

She laid a total of six eggs.

causing the female to incubate more frequently than normal. In previous years, she had begun incubation in earnest with the laying of the fourth egg, but this particular year she was brooding two eggs as though she had a full clutch. However, when one day turned out hot and sunny she spent much time off the nest, only settling down on them in the evening.

With the laying of the fourth egg, I sent off an order for ten aluminium closed rings, suitable for Sparrowhawks. It is preferable, if not always desirable, to close-ring any hawks bred in captivity. It is now compulsory to ring aviary-bred birds of prey with specially sized and coded Department of the Environment rings under the Wildlife and Countryside Act, for, not only can these be legally sold on the open market but it also gives the DoE some means of 'proving' that the birds have been captive produced. I place the word 'proving' in inverted commas, because the system has been abused by certain individuals in the past by ringing young birds in the nest and then taking them when they attain a suitable age, claiming the eyasses as aviary-bred. The new registration scheme should go a long way towards preventing this happening in the future, but at the time I am referring to, I was left with the only alternative, the time-honoured closed ringing system. This system was used by the now defunct 1954 Protection of Birds Act, which made it illegal to sell, or offer for sale, any British birds of prey unless they were aviary-bred and close-ringed.

I only had two choices of closed rings. One type was colour-coded for the year, red for 1981, and the other was ordinary plain, silver-coloured aluminium. I opted for the latter, not because they were cheaper, which they were, but because I felt that a red ring on a young hawk's leg would resemble a piece of meat and as such might attract the attention of another bird. There were enough problems involved without creating more. The rings arrived by return of post.

With the laying of the fifth egg, I set up the Turn-X incubator. I had planned to remove the first clutch a full seven days after the laying of the last egg, for, apparently, a period of natural incubation by the female prior to artificial incubation, greatly enhances the hatching percentage. Delaying too long can cause failure to reproduce and to lay a second clutch. However, with the cold weather, I decided to remove the first clutch seven days after the laying of the fourth egg. Before I could do this however, I had to ensure that the incubator was running correctly and had stabilised. To help in this matter, I created a temperature and relative humidity chart to monitor fluctuations by taking readings several times a day. My first discovery was that, with the Turn-X, monitoring of the humidity on the wet-bulb thermometer provided was virtually impossible, for the wick clogged with mineral salts, even from the de-ionised water I was using, causing the reading to soar to 100 per cent humidity, rather than the desired 40 per cent.

I telephoned Robin Haigh about this and he informed me that once the humidity has been established, the wick could be thrown away, although I kept the wick connected because its capillary action, when dipped into the base of the water-fountain outlet, drew up a supply of water into the incubator. Robin suggested that all I needed to do was to part fill the first chamber with water throughout the incubation period, flooding the bottom of the incubator once the eggs began to pip. I was surprised at the small volume of water required in the first chamber to produce a reading of 40 per cent. The temperature fluctuated very little, almost constantly remaining around 99° Fahrenheit.

On May 21, I entered the aviary, wearing a pair of thin rubber surgical gloves with which to handle the eggs, so as to reduce the possibility of transmitting any harmful bacteria to the eggs and thus to the incubator, where the heat and humidity would provide a superb environment for a bacteria culture. The incubator had been fumigated with Alphagen Prills, a formaldehyde-based fumigant, prior to placing the eggs in. There is evidence that fumigation is highly advisable and as a standard practice, I now fumigate my incubators before and after the breeding season.

I photographed the female with her eggs before attempting to remove them, whereupon she merely threatened me by raising her mantle feathers and calling defiantly. However, when I moved forward to take the eggs and place them in an egg-tray, she showed me no mercy. The rubber gloves that I had taken such pains to put on, were in tatters at the first assault and by the time the sixth egg was transferred to the box, my hands were so badly scratched that they became a welter of blood.

Before placing the eggs carefully in the incubator, I marked each one with an 'X' on one side and an 'O' on the other with a blue felt-tip pen. These were turning marks to enable me to ensure that each egg was receiving the same

The female Sparrowhawk raised her mantle feathers to threaten me.

number of turns as the others. Having marked them, each egg was positioned, pointed end slightly downwards, in individual compartments of the egg-turning frame. The turner itself was connected and switched on, then tested. All six eggs rolled perfectly and would now do so, automatically, 180° every hour, first one way, and then back again.

From then on, I became the typical expectant father. In fact, Jill unkindly remarked that I was more concerned over the hatching of my eggs than the birth of my own children! Unlike my own children, who had doctors, nurses, midwives, not to mention Jill and myself to care for them, the future of Sparrowhawk eggs lay entirely in my hands. Strangely enough, I became choked with guilt over removing the eggs from the adult female and when she settled down to brood an empty nest that evening, I felt a real heel. A well-meaning friend suggested that I give her a few pot eggs to incubate. Of course this was not on, because the whole purpose of removing the entire first clutch was to stimulate production of a second, an egg of any description, pot or otherwise, would be enough to prevent her from recycling. To be sure, I was not certain that the pair would recycle, for it is known that not all hawks do automatically recycle after removal of the first clutch, whereas others will readily lay second and even third clutches. I would have to wait and see.

The recycling period varies from species to species, but according to records in my possession, the time allotted for the Sparrowhawk was ten to 12 days. After my robbery of her first clutch, it seemed to take a long time to restore her dignity and peace of mind. At least the day following the removal of the clutch she abandoned the practice of brooding the empty eyrie, although she was still sullen and paid little attention to me when I observed her behaviour through the spy-hole.

Then, three days later, she resumed her arrogant disposition by hecking loudly at my intrusion, followed by an attack of unprecedented ferocity. This I took to be a good sign that she was resuming breeding condition. Ten days came and went, as did 12, with still no signs of an egg. However, on the 11th day she did begin brooding the same nest in the elderberry tree. She sat tightly for three full days before laying the first egg of the second clutch on June 4, a full 14 days after the removal of the first clutch.

The production of this egg was remarkable in that of the grand total of 19 eggs laid so far by this particular bird, this was the first to be laid in the afternoon, all others had been deposited during the early morning. That same evening, I candled the eggs of the first clutch. Candling is the process whereby an egg is held up to a strong light in a darkened room to determine fertility. Having never candled an egg before, I was only vaguely aware of what I was looking for, and because of their thick, chalky shells, Sparrowhawks eggs are not easy to candle. Undaunted, however, I set up my slide-projector in the bedroom and waited until after dark. I had previously covered up the bulk of the lens by placing black tape over the lens-hood, leaving a space just slightly smaller than the eggs in order to concentrate the light source. Each egg was placed in turn in front of the lamp and I was amazed how hard I had to look to see anything. However, the air-space at the top of the egg was visible in all six eggs, but instead of the dark centre spot with a number of veins radiating outwards, as I had expected, all I could observe was a deep red mass filling the entire area below the air-space.

I was beginning to feel a trifle disappointed after the first five eggs were all of this nature, but it was not until I placed the sixth and final egg in front of the lamp and turned it slowly that I realised I was looking at a 'clear' or infertile egg, all the previous five were fertile! Although the air-space was visible in the clear egg, the area below it was as though it was filled with water. The 'deep red areas' I had been looking at were indeed well-developed embryos.

In the meantime, the adult female continued to produce her second clutch, laying the remainder on June 7, June 9, and the fourth and final egg on June 11. According to my literature on the subject, most second clutches are smaller in number than the first and this was certainly so in my case, but apart from that, these eggs were virtually indistinguishable from the first six. So, with a grand total of ten eggs for the season, I was in with a good chance and I remembered saying to Jill that if I could only rear just one, I would be more than satisfied.

Usually, if a first clutch is fertile, it generally follows that the second will be also, and in my case, I was fairly certain that it would be, for not only was the female brooding well and defending her territory, but so was the musket. Many are the times I watched him brooding the eggs while the female was away bathing or feeding, and on several occasions I saw them both brooding together, side by side. Never before had I heard of such behaviour. My sole regret was, that try as I might, I failed to obtain a photographic record of this 'double-brooding'. The remainder of the project I photographed diligently, producing a very interesting selection of colour slides for use in my lectures.

The brooding process back in the incubator seemed interminable. The books stated that the incubation period for the Sparrowhawk was 33 to 35 days. To me it seemed more like 33 years, but finally, on the morning of June 14, the first egg pipped. I was ecstatic. There were two well-defined bumps, bang on the 'X' turning mark. I knew from reading up that once an egg begins to pip, the turning process is discontinued. However, there were five more eggs in the incubator which had not yet pipped and therefore, still required the turning motion. I had already planned ahead for this asynchronous hatching and had borrowed a Hova-bator incubator from a falconer friend who was not using it at the time. The Hova-bator I set up with full humidity and with a temperature of 98° Fahrenheit. The high humidity is crucial at this stage in order to prevent the shell membranes from drying out, so stopping the chick from revolving inside and chipping its way out with its egg-tooth.

The period from pipping to hatching can be considerable, for, once pipped, the chick often rests up for hours at a time, sometimes taking as much as 80 hours to complete the process. All I could do was to place the egg, pipped side uppermost in the incubator and continue to make periodic checks.

Luckily, I had my hatching dates timed to almost perfection, for I had booked two weeks of my annual leave from work to care for the chicks. I had planned to hand-rear the first clutch and allow the parents to bring up the second. This way, I could obtain partially imprinted, relatively tame hawks for flying purposes from the first clutch, and wild, but aviary environmentally orientated hawks to plough back into the breeding programme. I had discovered that hawks reared in an aviary environment are much more likely to breed in captivity than trapped, imported birds. The reasons for this are as obscure as they are varied, but possibly the two most important factors are stress, although skylight- and seclusion-type aviaries largely eliminate this, and the well-known ornithological fact that young hawks reared on, say, a cliff nest-site for example, are more prone to return to such a site for the rearing of their own broods rather than in a tree and vice versa. I believe that in the same

Top left *X marks the spot. Pipping of the first egg on June 14.*

Top right *The hole gradually lengthens and cheeping sounds can be heard from within the egg-shell.*

Above left *As the chick revolves around inside the shell, the cracks, or pip-marks form a line around the wide end.*

Above right *Sparrowhawk chick displays his egg-tooth on the end of his beak.*

context, a hawk reared in an aviary is not averse to breeding in one.

There was still no change in the pipped egg by the following morning, although cheeping sounds could be heard from within the shell. This cheeping sound was audible right across the bedroom, where I had set up the incubator. By this time, a second egg had also pipped, this too being transferred to the Hova-bator. A third egg had been observed rolling about without the aid of the automatic turning device.

At 1:50 on the morning of June 16, I was awakened by loud and frequent

Above and above right *The chick is exhausted after its efforts and rests awhile, then proceeds to remove the shell.* **Right** *Freed from the shell at last.*

cheeping sounds coming from the Hova-bator, especially when the red thermostat pilot light came on and lit up the interior. I lay awake a few moments gathering my wits, before climbing out of bed to lift up the lid of the incubator. There, to my utmost joy, I saw that the first chick had all but hatched, only the extreme tip of its rear-end remained within the shell. It had chipped around the shell from the pipping point and taken the top off the egg like a door.

I had hoped to take a series of photographs of the hatching procedure, but I was only half awake and very probably would not have even been able to *find* the camera, let alone assemble and use it. There were other eggs to hatch and I just hoped that one of them would be so courteous as to hatch at a respectable hour. I arose at 6:30 to find that not only had the chick dried off nicely, but the second chick had hatched also. This one was still wet, so I believed its emergence had been within the hour. The first chick was fed shortly afterwards and then both were fed every two to three hours throughout the day.

For the first day's feed, I removed all bone, feathers and fur from the meat but, thereafter, they were fed with the roughage added. On June 17, I watched and photographed the hatching of the third chick. It was at this stage in the proceedings that I realised a third incubator was a necessity, for it was too humid in the Hova-bator for the hatched chicks. The problem was partly solved by placing all the eggs in the Hova-bator and turning the unpipped ones manually, while the Turn-X top was placed on to a specially made plywood

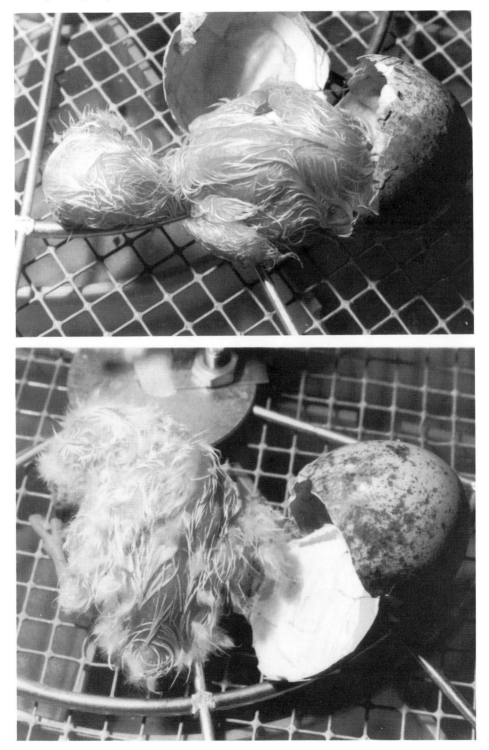

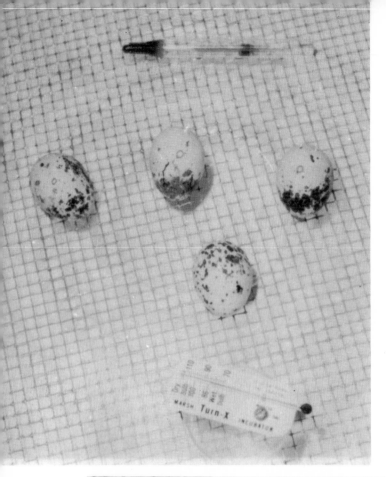

Left *I placed all the eggs in the Hova-bator and turned the unpipped ones manually.*

Below *The second chick hatched shortly after the first.*

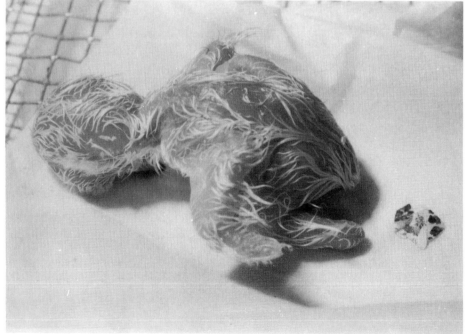

Right *One chick had dried off nicely, but the other was still wet.*

Below *I placed a thermometer in the brooder.*

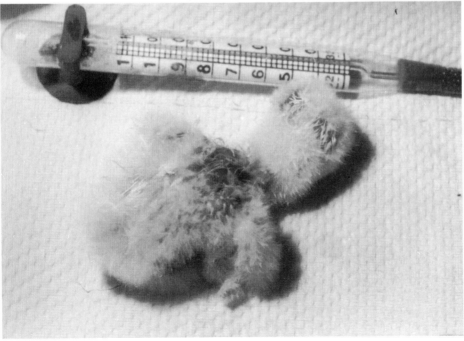

Above *The chicks on a layer of kitchen towels.*

Below *By the evening of June 18, four chicks had seen the light of day.*

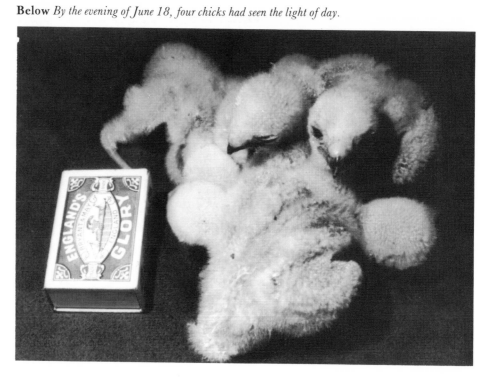

I ringed the two eldest chicks.

box, adapted to take the circular base of the incubator dome. I placed a thermometer in the box after fumigation and once it had stabilised at 98°, the chicks were placed inside on a layer of paper kitchen towels. By the evening of June 18, four chicks had seen their first light of day. To identify each individual, I colour-coded them by marking each right leg with a felt-tip pen. The first hatched was marked blue, the second green, the third I left with no mark at all while the fourth was daubed with black.

On June 26, I ringed the two eldest chicks, both of whom were females and on the 28th I ringed the youngest, again a female. The third one I could not ring until the 29th, as this was the only musket in the brood and thus smaller. I dissected the fifth egg for it had gone well past its alloted pipped date and found inside, a fully-formed, but dead chick. The only theory that I can offer for its death is that possibly it had received too much humidity too soon by placing it in the Hova-bator with the pipped eggs. I took grim notice of this fact and decided to acquire more incubators for the next season. This sort of thing must not happen again.

The four chicks were growing rapidly and by July 7, the first egg of the second clutch had hatched under the female. I could not believe my good fortune. The acid test now was: would she rear them? The following day, I checked in the aviary to find out if all was well with the young chick when I observed that one of the eggs was missing. For a moment, several things ran through my mind. Was I looking at a second chick and had the first chick been

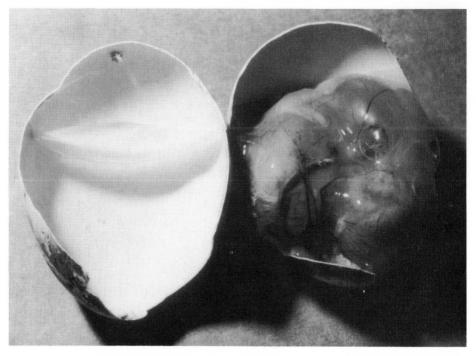

Above *The fifth egg. Inside, a fully-formed, but dead chick.*

Below *A Sparrowhawk chick resting.*

Sparrowhawk chicks beneath an electric hen brooder.

eaten, or had it fallen from the nest? One way or another, I had to know. So I ventured into the aviary, warding off attacks from the female. There was nothing on the ground beneath the nest and it was only by mere chance that I glanced into the tray where I had deposited the other nest, which was also last season's nesting site but now used as the musket's plucking post. There, in the depression and resting on the pine needles, was the missing egg! It was stone cold and had a small hole in the shell in the air-space section. I removed it from the aviary and placed it in a dish in my study for the morning, for my holiday was over and I had to return to work.

At lunch time I came home and, at Jill's suggestion, began to open up the egg at the pipping point to determine the contents of the egg. Carefully, I used pointed forceps to remove small pieces of shell until, with amazement, I detected a movement. There was a live, fully-formed chick inside, but the membranes were drying up rapidly. The incubators had been dismantled as the chicks in the first clutch were now without need of heat; they had been acclimatised gradually by turning down the temperature daily until they could easily withstand normal room temperature and could be kept in a large cardboard box instead of a brooder. It would take too long to stabilise an incubator for this little chick, so the only alternative was to place it back beneath the female. Luckily, she had just had a bath and her wet feathers would, I hoped, be sufficient to moisten the membranes and allow the chick to hatch normally, although I must confess, I held out little hope for its survival. How it came to

Above *On July 10, the chick from the abandoned egg hatched.*
Below *The female prepares to defend her chicks.*
Above right *She advances to the edge of the nest before launching her assault.*
Right *Even when her chicks have attained a more advanced age, the female will attack and scream.*

be in the other nest at the opposite end of the aviary is a complete mystery. Obviously, one of the parent birds placed it there, but why? Why incubate it for the full term and then on the very day it pipped, move it? This captive breeding was raising some questions that I would previously never have dreamt of asking.

I checked the egg in the evening. The chick was still very much alive but I suffered a terrific battering from the female. She grabbed me by the head and pummelled my scalp with her needle sharp talons, drawing blood in numerous places. The pain was excruciating, but I could thank my lucky stars that she was only a diminutive Sparrowhawk and not a Golden Eagle. The following day, the chick could be seen vigorously moving about through the hole in the shell, only this time I observed from outside the aviary. I also watched the female tenderly feeding the hatched chick. Such a transformation from the raging demon of yesterday.

Finally, on July 10, the chick from the abandoned egg hatched. To me, it was little short of a miracle. The third and final chick of this clutch hatched the following day, the fourth egg being clear. These chicks turned out to be two females and a musket, making a grand total of five females and two muskets. Far more than I had expected in all my wildest dreams. Not only had I succeeded, but more importantly, I had learnt so much from the project. I had

I selected the largest female from the first clutch and named her Zulu (I. Overton).

Young Sparrowhawks being hand-reared together to partially imprint them.

enough hawks to set up another programme, enough to fly, and a superb set of coloured slides of the entire procedure, so that I could relive time and again, the magical moments of the 1981 breeding season.

At last, I was self-sufficient and could realise my personal ambition, to fly at natural quarry, my own home-bred raptors. Ever since the mid-1960s I had been nursing that dream, now all that remained was to choose an eyas from the batch I hand-reared, train and fly it, and subsequently catch something with it. I chose the largest female from the first clutch, naming her 'Zulu', after a strong interest that I had developed over the years on the powerful inhabitants of south-east Africa, the mighty Zulu nation. From early on, I fed her by hand to partially imprint her. I do not believe in fully imprinting any hawk deliberately, that is, totally hand-rearing one bird and segregating it from its own kind so that it only sees its human foster parent. This initially instills into the hawk a parental affection towards its handler, but usually, when the hawk matures, this develops into a sexual response, so that the bird will perform sexual motions when the handler approaches, such as lowering of the head, raising of the tail feathers and calling, but rejecting advances from its own kind.

This sort of behaviour is useful for artificial insemination projects, a science which should be resorted to only by those fully experienced in the techniques involved, but it is a totally undesirable trait in all other aspects. Firstly, most *full* imprints are inveterate screamers, and, as such, are extremely irritating, but even more important is the sad fact that such hawks can seldom be used in further captive-breeding attempts other than artificial insemination. All such attempts known to me personally have failed miserably on account of extreme aggressive behaviour. In the same context, it will be noted from the foregoing that attempts at liberation back to the wild of such hawks are a complete waste of time and will probably result in the bird being shot when it tries to approach humans, with whose form the bird is well associated, while searching for food.

Personally, I would never imprint, or partially imprint anything other than a Sparrowhawk, as I believe that only handlers of the Sparrowhawk, or its foreign allied counterparts (not Goshawks) actually gain anything by their charges being *partially* imprinted. Partial imprinting is the hand-rearing of a number of hawks which are kept together right through until fledging. Such hawks show a marked degree of interest in, and affection for, the falconer, but are not so far imprinted that in future breeding projects they neglect their natural partners in preference for human ones. In short, the falconer is able to train and fly his partially imprinted Sparrowhawk with the chances of losing it in the field greatly reduced through its comparative tameness, and should the bird begin to scream, the noise in this species is negligible compared with most of the larger hawks and falcons. Also, at the end of the season, if so desired, the falconer is usually able to pair the bird up with its natural partner. This is what I planned for Zulu.

Compared with the passage or haggard Sparrowhawk, I found the partial imprint a sheer joy to fly and, despite being reared on a diet of chopped rats, mice and chicks, Zulu showed no qualms over flying natural quarry. From previous experience with instinctive behaviour in eyasses, it came as no great surprise to me that Zulu took eight head of quarry during her first season, including a moorhen and such formidable quarry as a weasel, which bit her several times during the course of the struggle. In fact, I have become so impressed with the partial imprint Sparrowhawk that I have flown two individuals throughout the past two seasons, with very encouraging results. In company with two colleagues, Peter Hudson and Martin Nicholson, both ardent Sparrowhawk fans, I have enjoyed some of the most exciting and, at times, comical, hawking of my entire career. The fact that these Sparrowhawks have all been captive-produced means they almost refuse to become lost, while an abundance of local quarry precludes the necessity of having to travel to remote corners both serving to enhance the delight attained by flying one of these deadly little hawks.

Towards the end of March, Tyne Tees Television telephoned me with a view towards making a film on falconry for their children's television programme, 'Madabout', featuring people who are mad about their particular hobby. This led to a meeting a few days later with the Programme Researcher Lesley Oakden. The programme was presented by Matthew Kelly of 'Game for a Laugh' fame. A date for the film crew to visit us was set for May 7.

Just prior to the filming date however, a major set-back occurred. Ajax hit a fence while flying and damaged her wing to such an extent that she could not

Zulu caught a moorhen during her first season.

fly. As soon as she attempted to fly to me, the wing buckled and she came to earth with a bump. I had no alternative other than to temporarily ground her. I contacted Tyne Tees Television to inform them of the problem, but as I had Zulu flying and Jill was using a buzzard, they still wished to go ahead as planned, using Ajax on the fist for fill-in shots.

On the very day we were to begin filming, I had to take Ajax to the vet's to have her wing X-rayed. Two X-rays were taken and they revealed that the wing was neither broken nor dislocated, as I had feared. There was some fibrous tissue around the joint, indicating that it may at some stage have been almost dislocated and healed up, whereupon the recent collision with the fence could have re-inflamed it. The vet thought the future for Ajax was none too bright, but time would tell. I had to apply 'Demavet' to the inflamed area daily for two weeks to reduce the inflammation.

Shortly after my arrival home from the vets, the film crew, together with Matthew Kelly, arrived at our home. It was quite a thrill having Matthew in our house after seeing him so many times on television and I was amazed at how tall he was. He was a great character who took a real interest in everything we did.

The cameramen filmed Ajax, Zulu and the buzzard in the garden, together with my breeding pair of Sparrowhawks who were incubating three eggs and my recently acquired breeding pair of Arctic Snowy Owls. The venue for the flying sequences was on a field just across the road from our house, where

nowadays I begin the training of most of my birds. We began by filming Matthew holding Ajax, then our daughter Joanne flying Zulu to my fist, then Joanne flying Zulu to Matthew and vice versa. Zulu played her part to perfection. An interview was then conducted between Matthew and myself, finally ending the sequence with Jill flying her buzzard, which also performed impeccably. The whole film took several hours to complete but it was an experience we all enjoyed to the full. The film turned out well and was shown on 'Madabout' early in 1984.

After the breeding season, I selected a Sparrowhawk from the first clutch of the 1982 breeding programme. Again I chose a female, the only female in the brood of five, and named her, in exceedingly poor taste I hasten to admit, Exocet. She was hatched at the time of the Falklands conflict and was named

Left *Ajax was filmed in the garden by the* Madabout *film crew, Tyne Tees Television* (Madabout, Tyne Tees Television).

Below left *We began by filming Matthew Kelly holding Ajax* (Madabout, Tyne Tees Television).

Below *My daughter, Joanne, flew Zulu the Sparrowhawk to Matthew Kelly's fist and vice-versa* (Madabout, Tyne Tees Television).

Above left *An interview was conducted between Matthew Kelly and myself. Matthew is seen here holding Zulu the Sparrowhawk* (Madabout, Tyne Tees Television).

Left *Ajax endured the cameras of Tyne Tees Television hooded . .* (Madabout, Tyne Tees Television).

Above *. . . as well as un-hooded* (Madabout, Tyne Tees television).

Right *We all enjoyed working with Matthew Kelly and the* Madabout *team. Left to right: Joanne, Matthew, Jill with her buzzard, myself with Zulu and David Jnr* (Madabout, Tyne Tees Television).

Exocet, with tail-bell and taped tail, was hatched during the Falklands conflict.

after the lethal missiles used by Argentina during that war, hoping that she would prove as deadly an adversary towards quarry as the now infamous missiles were to our fleet. I certainly had no need to fear on that score, for she killed a sparrow at the mere age of 21 days. Although the latter was unintentional on my part, it shed light on important aspects of early instinctive behaviour in the Sparrowhawk. I had read in *Eagles, Hawks and Falcons of the World*, by Leslie Brown and Dean Amadon, that the *urge* to kill in young Sparrowhawks does not develop until they are at least 50 days of age. These facts no doubt arising from observations at wild eyries where the dead, often headless victims are brought in to feed the young, providing them with no opportunity to even *see*, let alone attempt to kill, a live bird.

At 21 days of age, a young Sparrowhawk is able to run about and has many feathers protruding through the thick white down. My first clutch of 1982 were at this stage when I turned them loose in a small outside flight to give them the benefit of the early morning sunshine. The flight was planted with elderberry to provide shade and shelter and for some weeks, being unoccupied, the door had been left ajar. Unknown to me, a sparrow had flown in prior to placing the eyasses inside, but the chicks soon spotted it and gave chase. It was efficiently caught and despatched by Exocet who, until that point, had never before seen another bird of any description other than her own nest-mates. I witnessed the final stages of the killing and can without a shred of doubt confirm that the urge to kill is certainly apparent at 21 days, less than half the age advocated by Brown and Amadon. The remaining four muskets made numerous attempts to rob Exocet of her kill.

However, in all fairness to the noted authors, my situation was a synthetic one which would be highly unlikely to occur in the wild state. Nevertheless, it does demonstrate that previously unresearched and hitherto unknown facts relating to wild hawks can often be discovered by breeding birds in a captive environment.

Exocet was trained and on the wing by September 1, the date when my new

Exocet, aged 21 days. I discovered that the urge to kill is already apparent in this species at this age.

Above *Instinctive behaviour. The 1982 clutch of young Sparrowhawks pose on the lawn.*

Below *However, the instant the sun shone upon them, they all simultaneously spread their wings to catch the warmth.*

licence to catch blackbirds with a trained hawk was to commence. The blackbird is the traditional quarry for the Sparrowhawk, but of course, the blackbird is a protected species and a Department of the Environment licence must be applied for, and received, before hawking begins. Provided the Sparrowhawk to be used is a legal specimen, the Department of the Environment will normally issue a licence to take 25 blackbirds per season. Now, 25 blackbirds may not seem many to the layman, but any experienced falconer knows only too well that the taking of such a number of blackbirds is no mean feat. The lethargic looking blackbird tugging at a worm on the garden lawn is a very different prospect when being pursued by a Sparrowhawk. Suffice it to say that the blackbird has earned my respect on numerous occasions, and I have an exceptionally high regard for the species. On more times than I care to remember one solitary blackbird has completely outwitted no less than three Sparrowhawks sent against it and through superb tactics left each hawk in turn in a confused and befuddled state.

While in the midst of flying Exocet, my daughter Joanne had written to the BBC Television Centre in London. A new programme was beginning on Saturday mornings to replace Noel Edmonds 'Multicoloured Swapshop'. This programme was to be entitled 'Saturday Superstore', and presented by Mike Read, Keith Chegwin and John Craven. The programme was designed to feature items especially asked for by the viewers and the BBC had asked for viewers' ideas on suitable topics. This is where Joanne came on the scene.

Exocet, almost fully fledged.

The fact that a few individuals kept eagles in their back gardens intrigued the BBC's Saturday Superstore *team.*

Unknown to the rest of us, she duly sent off a letter explaining about our rare Imperial Eagle, and then, believing that she would hear nothing further, promptly forgot all about the affair.

Shortly afterwards, the telephone rang and I answered it. Cathy Gilbey of the BBC was on the other end of the line and, having heard all about our eagle from Joanne, was now sounding out whether or not I would be prepared to take the bird to the studios when the programme began in October. After the initial shock had worn off, I agreed to take Ajax to the studios in London. I had been on the look-out for a mate for Ajax for some time and hoped that someone with a male may see the programme and get in touch, although I knew that there were very few Imperial Eagles in the country. In fact, I believe it was this latter aspect which attracted the BBC, together with the fact that there were in existence individuals like myself who kept such creatures in their back gardens.

On the very first broadcast of 'Saturday Superstore', a live programme, Mike Read phoned Joanne at our home to ask if she would like to come on the show the following week with myself and Ajax. Joanne gladly accepted. During the middle of the following week, the BBC rang us to give directions to the studios and to inform us that we were to appear, live, at 10:17 am, but requested us to arrive as early as possible for pre-programme briefing. They also asked for details on falconry and in particular, the Imperial Eagle. We were all very excited at the prospect of visiting the famous studios at Wood Lane.

On Saturday, October 9, the alarm went at 4 am, and by 6 am, we, that is, Jill, Joanne, our son David, Ajax and I were all on the long drive to the television studios in London. Security staff on the gates directed us to Studio 7, from which 'Saturday Superstore' is broadcast and where technicians were already laying out cables and setting up lights in preparation for the morning's programme. There were a great many more people and much more equipment behind the scenes than I had ever realised.

We were met by a secretary and escorted to dressing-room 206 where I tethered Ajax to her cadge and stored our equipment. Another secretary paid us a visit while I sorted out our gear and supplied us with a welcome cup of coffee and a copy of the morning's script. Signed photographs of Mike Read, John Craven, Maggie Philbin, Keith Chegwin and David Icke were presented to Joanne and David and we were then invited to sit in the 'coffee-shop' section of the Superstore set to watch the morning's programme and await our cue to go on the air. Mike Read was already in his 'managers' chair a few feet away from us, while Keith Chegwin and John Craven floated about the studio finalising last minute details.

Joanne and I were cued to take up our positions in area 'F', the 'Pet Department' with Ajax. Here I set up the equipment I had specially brought along, namely the trusty Turn-X incubator that had served me so well, a Sioux-style American Indian warbonnet and shield that I had made from Ajax's moulted feathers, spare gauntlets, hoods and other falconry paraphernalia. Mike Read came over from interviewing 'Photostat', a dance team, and for several minutes, with studio cameras trained on us and with an estimated audience of some 20 million people, I answered Mike's questions. I would have thought that after so many lectures, displays and other public appearances, a live television broadcast would not have affected me too much, but, although it apparently didn't show on screen, I was extremely nervous and the palms of my hands ran with sweat. Part way through the interview we were joined by Keith Chegwin who provided a spot of humour and then we had a short break while an excerpt of eagles in flight, taken from the *Flight of the Condor* series, was shown on video tape.

After the show, Frances Ommanney, assistant producer and outside broadcast director for 'Saturday Superstore' showed us all round the studio, including the 'nerve centre' which was a forest of monitors, lights, dials, faders and other broadcasting equipment. At the time, I had no way of knowing that Frances and I would be meeting again before very long.

At mid-day, when the programme went off the air to make way for 'Grandstand', Jill, the children and I joined the presentation staff and stars for a buffet lunch in one of the many rooms of the television centre at Wood Lane.

Above *A short clip of Ajax has been included in the leader to* Saturday Superstore, *and is shown at the beginning of every programme of that series.*

Below *Keith Chegwin, Peter Hudson with Sparrowhawk and Martin Nicholson during filming for the BBC's* Saturday Superstore.

The author with his male Snowy Owl.

I well remember looking round the room at all those famous faces and would never have dreamed that the original ownership of Winky the Little Owl could eventually have led to all this.

Halfway through November, Frances Ommanney phoned me from London. She wanted to film a follow-up to our appearance on 'Saturday Superstore'. In fact, since we appeared on the programme, a short clip of Ajax's head and shoulders had been included in the leader and shown at the beginning of every programme ever since. I arranged a date with Frances to come to our home and discuss the possibilities of making the film.

Frances came up from London one Sunday afternoon, when we spent some five hours sorting out the pros and cons of the film. At that stage in the proceedings, a presenter had not been decided upon, but Frances felt that Keith Chegwin would probably get the job. Two days had been allocated to complete the film and a script would have to be written before any filming could begin. I suggested to Frances that if we could include Peter Hudson and Martin Nicholson with their two Sparrowhawks, as well as Ajax and Exocet, not to mention the Snowy Owls that I had in a breeding project, then we stood

Male Snowy Owl in breeding enclosure.

a better chance of obtaining more flying shots from the three Sparrowhawks than from my single bird. Frances was quite happy to include my colleagues, as I explained from past experience, that to guarantee the performance of one individual bird on any given day was tantamount to courting disaster. With using three birds, the chances of one performing well on the day placed the odds more in our favour. In the meantime, I chose Trent Fields as the location for our film debut and had to obtain written permission from the Seven Trent Water Authority to take a BBC film crew on their property.

Towards the end of December, however, I suffered a major set-back. Exocet collapsed and died from unknown causes shortly after I tethered her to the bow-perch early one morning. I was shattered. She had been a superb little hawk and I was also counting on her to use in the BBC film. Ajax's wing was still suspect and I had been resting her since the 'Madabout' film. The Superstore film date had been set for January 11 and 12 and I only had a few days left in which to reclaim her and put her on the wing again. It was

Female Snowy Owl in breeding enclosure.

impossible, but I informed Frances that I would do my best, for I could not get the film postponed to a later date. The scripts had already gone out and a film crew assigned. I would do my utmost but could not afford to take Ajax's weight down too rapidly without seriously risking her health, and that I would never do. The condition of her wing was an unknown quantity too.

Ajax soon began to fly short distances and to my everlasting joy, her injured wing had healed perfectly. My nagging worry now was that I doubted very much if I could persuade her to fly suitably long distances for filming. By mid-morning on January 11, Frances Ommanney and her secretary for the film, Debbie Searle, arrived at our home, closely followed by Keith Chegwin, who was to be the presenter. Having two well-known people in our house within a matter of months was a novel and unique experience for us.

The venue for the first afternoon's filming was Trent Fields, although the first sequences were taken of loading the hawks into our cars, Keith Chegwin joining Joanne and I in our car and setting off for the fields. The weather was

Close-up of female Snowy Owl.

overcast, exceptionally windy and bitterly cold, not good for hawks, cameras or sound recording. I was fitted with a radio microphone clipped to my tie, and although the sound recording went well, despite the harsh wind, Peter and Martin's two Sparrowhawks suffered from the turbulent air and Ajax flatly refused to fly. She was too interested in the activities of the film crew. As darkness fell and we packed up our gear for the day, I felt somewhat embarrassed and remembered the show business saying 'never work with children or animals'. At least, I was thankful that we had another day at our disposal. Keith at least remained cheerful, as he always is.

At 9 am the following morning, the film crew assembled at our home where filming began immediately. Most of the morning was spent filming Keith, Joanne and myself taking Ajax and Martin's Sparrowhawk out of the mews and on to the weathering lawn, then weighing both birds on their respective sets of scales, showing hawking gear and its use and imping a new primary feather into the left wing of Peter's Sparrowhawk. At the end of this session I was thoroughly amazed at the length of time that had elapsed while filming these relatively short and simple sequences. However, enough time remained to attempt more flying sequences, but again, high winds posed a problem whereby none of the hawks were prepared to fly more than short distances, spending more time perched high up in tall trees. Ajax, for the first time ever, jumped onto Keith Chegwin's gloved fist, where we conducted an interview sequence. A few more flying shots concluded the film, when we all returned to the warm comforts of our home for a welcome dinner prepared by Jill.

There was no time to film the Snowy Owls and at the back of my mind was the nagging feeling that we were sadly lacking in suitable flying shots. It had not worked out quite as I had hoped, but at least, now that the film had been completed, I could relax a little. After lunch, I drove Keith to Nottingham Midland Station for he had to catch the mid-afternoon train to London in time for Tony Blackburn's radio show. As if to add insult to injury, the Sparrowhawks performed impeccably at quarry the following weekend, and within a fortnight, Ajax was flying superbly at distances of up to 200 yards.

In the meantime, Frances had the film developed and telephoned to inform me that it had come out well, but as expected, more flying shots were needed so we would at least have another opportunity to redeem our hawks' flying skills. A date at the end of March was set to finalise the film for the BBC, and as no sound was required, only Frances, a cameraman and assistant cameraman would be present. We had to wear the identical clothing to that worn on the filming date some two months previously, for continuity reasons, but at least, I felt more confident that this time we should acquire some suitable film in the can.

Ajax flatly refused to fly.

Above left *Ajax jumped on to Keith Chegwin's fist.*

Left *For the flying sequences for* Saturday Superstore, *Ajax was required to fly from her perch . .*

Above *. . . over the open field . . .*

Below *. . . to land upon my gauntlet.*

Continuity shots of Ajax's leash, bells and feet were required.

A few continuity shots in the mews, of Ajax's leash and both Ajax and Martin's Sparrowhawk on the weathering lawn were filmed first of all, Peter's Sparrowhawk having since been placed in a breeding project. This time, although her flying was well below her usual standard, together with the fact that she took her own sweet time in returning to the gauntlet, about eight separate flights were filmed, mostly in slow-motion. For variety, she was flown from a bow-perch, a football goal-post and finally from Peter's fist to mine.

At the end of a long morning's filming, I felt that we had finally redeemed ourselves and that the completed film would certainly benefit from the extra day. A letter from Frances a few days later confirmed the latter and I felt much happier. The finished result, when screened at the beginning of the second series, lasted some ten minutes or so, but I doubt if many viewers realised that it all took so long to film and caused me so much worry and concern.

*   *   *

Ajax sits hooded in the back of the car, her bells tinkling in the half light of early morning. Soon, in the company of a few good friends, I will be out in the fields and fresh air enjoying a sport which for me has become not so much a hobby but more a way of life. Ares the Steppe Eagle, has gone into a breeding programme, but after 14 years, Ajax is still strong on the wing and will be for a good many more to come, I hope. I wait patiently for the arrival of my colleagues, so that once again Ajax can thrill us with her masterful rabbit-chasing antics over the autumn stubble. As for next season? Well, plans are already in motion. New incubators are on order and as captive breeding becomes more and more sophisticated, I am forever on the look-out for new techniques and ideas. The patter of baby Snowy Owl feet is very much on my mind, and if only I could obtain a mate for Ajax!

I hope that the contents of this book have given the reader an insight into the fascinating world of the falconer and have shown some of the reasons why my blood runs more quickly at the sight of a hawk. For it is entirely due to raptors that I have visited so many interesting places and met literally thousands of wonderful people.

Photography and wildlife filming has become an important part of my life and as a result, I have built up a collection of colour transparencies covering the majority of my interests, from obscure fungi in deep woodlands, to beautiful tropical butterflies and moths which I rear annually in a purpose-built greenhouse. But as rewarding as these hobbies certainly are, they have been unable to compete with my first love, the noble art of falconry. The sport has been like a drug within me, I could not shake off its effects even if I wanted to.

My friends have arrived, the hawks are already in the cars, who knows what adventures we now face. Will we catch anything? With this sport it does not really matter if we don't. Will a hawk be lost? We certainly hope not, but with hawking, one can never tell, which is probably one reason for making it all the more exciting. So, towards the wild rugged moorlands we go, perhaps some day, you too would like to join us.

For the future, I hope that I will always be able to refer to my garden as a 'Garden of Eagles'.

Appendix

The following addresses were correct at the time of writing. However, in due course some of these may change, particularly in the case of club secretaries. When writing to any of these bodies, it is worth remembering to enclose a stamped addressed envelope.

Equipment
John Cox
Taly-coed Court
Nr Monmouth
Gwent
(Books and Equipment)

Martin Jones
The Lodge
Huntley
Gloucestershire
(Books and Equipment)

Northampton Falconry Services
27 Willow Lane
Great Houghton
Northampton
(Books, Equipment and Hawk Food)

Robin Haigh
Colonels Lane
Abbeybridge Farmhouse
Chertsey
Surrey
(Books, Equipment and Incubators)

Applications for licences
—To import birds of prey.
—To take a hawk from the wild for purposes of falconry.
—To take blackbirds with trained Sparrowhawks.
—To take skylarks with trained Merlins etc.

Department of the Environment
Wildlife Conservation Licensing Section
Tollgate House
Houlton Street
Bristol BS2 9DJ

Scottish Home and Health Department
Room 343
St Andrew's House
Edinburgh EH1 3DE

Falconry centres
The following offer courses on falconry and/or, weather permitting, demonstrations of free-flying birds of prey.

The Falconry Centre
Newent
Gloucestershire
GL18 1JJ

The World of Wings
Bird Garden and Falconry Club
Kilnsea
Hull
North Humberside

Robert Haddon
Broomhill House
71 Lutterworth Road
Burbage
Hinckley
Leicestershire

Welsh Hawking Centre
Weycock Road
Barry
South Glamorgan
Wales CF6 9AA

The Hawk Conservancy
Weyhill
Andover
Hampshire SP11 8DY

West Midlands Falconry Centre
c/o Brian Patterson
Rose Acre Garden Centre
Kidderminster Road South
West Hagley
Worcestershire

Chris and Emma Ford
British School of Falconry
Stelling Minnis
Canterbury
Kent CT4 6AQ

Clubs and associations

The British Falconer's Club
c/o P.T. Fields
3 Orchard Lane
Longton
Preston PR4 5AX
(Publication: *The Falconer*)

The Northern England Falconers Club
c/o B. Thelwell
2 Fourlands Drive
Lolle
Bradford
Yorkshire BD10 9SJ

The Welsh Hawking Club
c/o Ann Shuttleworth
21 North Close
Blackfordby
Burton-on-Trent
Staffs DE11 8AP
(Publication: *The Austringer*)

The Raptor Breeders Association
c/o The Falconry Centre
Newent
Gloucestershire

The North Staffordshire Falconers Club
Mrs Barbara Chadwick
59 Little Moss
Scholar Green
Kidsgrove
Staffs

Glossary

Falconry has a jargon all its own, some of which is still used in our everyday English language. Listed below is a selection from this colourful terminology.

Arms The legs of a hawk from thigh to foot.

Austringer The trainer of short-winged hawks, ie, Goshawk and Sparrowhawk.

Aylmeri Leather anklets or bracelets, often used today on small hawks as an improvement on the traditional jesses. Named after its inventor, Major Guy Aylmer.

Ayre or *Eyrie* The nesting place of a bird of prey.

Bate To fly or flutter from the fist or perch, usually a predominant feature of an untrained hawk.

Barak Decoy hawk fitted with nooses to trap other hawks. A device used commonly in Asia and the Arab world.

Beam Feathers The phalangeal or primary wing feathers.

Bechins A small morsel of food—a beakful.

Bewits Strips of leather by which the bells are fastened to the legs; several types, ie, traditional, button or even the modern plastic cable tie has been used with success.

Bind To catch and hold the quarry in mid-air (to bind to).

Block A truncated, or cylindrical wooden perch upon which a falcon is normally tethered for daily weathering.

Blood feathers New feathers still growing and being fed by a blood supply. Such feathers will bleed profusely if damaged at this stage.

Bolt, to fly at To fly at quarry straight from the fist, as in short-winged hawks.

Bowiser A young hawk able to fly from bough to bough of its nest tree.

Bowse To drink (also spelt bouse, boose, bouze and booze), hence our slang term of today for partaking of intoxicating liquor.

Bow-perch A semi-circular perch fixed into the ground, normally used for short-winged hawks. Somewhat resembling a long-bow in shape, hence the name.

Brail A soft pliable leather thong with a centre slit, used at one time for restraining an unruly bird by immobilising one wing. Nowadays used only for an ailing bird.

Brancher A more modern term for bowiser, a young hawk that has recently left the nest.

Break into Beginning to eat the kill.

Cadge The wooden rectangular frame on legs upon which hooded falcons are carried to the field by the cadger.

Cadger The person, often an apprentice falconer, who carries the cadge. This person often eked out a small income by telling interested spectators about his charges, for small tips. Hence cadger, a person who obtains something for very little. The word 'cad' is also said to derive from this.

Calling off To call the hawk to lure or fist from a post or branch.

Carriage The carrying of a hawk upon the fist in order to man it.

Carry, to To fly away from the falconer carrying the lure to kill.

Cast, to To immobilise a hawk while coping or jessing a hawk etc.

Cast, to To regurgitate a casting, or pellet.

Cast Two hawks together, flown as a cast, although not necessarily a true pair.

Cast gorge, to To bring up the undigested contents of the crop.

Cawking time Pairing time.

Cere The wax-like skin at the top of the beak (usually yellow) housing the nostrils.

Chanceleer To execute two or three sharp turns while stooping to lure or quarry.

Check, to fly at To fly at quarry different from that originally slipped at, or to leave one quarry and pursue another, perhaps easier one.

Cope To trim or pare overgrown beaks and talons.

Cowering Shaking or quivering of the wings in young hawks.

Crabbing When two hawks flown simultaneously fight, either in mid-air or on the ground.

Craye or cray A form of constipation in hawks.

Cramp A type of rickets, commonly seen in hand-reared young hawks, whereby through lack of experience, the young birds have received insufficient levels of calcium to aid growing bones.

Creance A long light line on which a bird is flown during training before it is trusted free.

Crines The short, hair-like feathers around the cere.

Croaks or kecks A respiratory disease, named after the sound the infected hawk makes after physical exertion, such as flying or bating.

Crop The dilatation of the gullet, or pouch, which serves as the first receptacle for the food taken by the hawk, prior to digestion.

Deck feathers The two centre feathers of the tail.

Draw the hood, to To draw the braces which facilitate the opening and closing of the hood.

Endew To put over the crop for digestion.

Enew To put into cover.

Enseam To purge a hawk of superfluous fat and bring it into flying condition.

Eyass, eyas A young hawk. If a hawk is taken as an eyas from the nest, it will, regardless of its age thereafter, be referred to as an eyass. Just the same as if the bird was taken as a passage or a haggard, the prefix remains with the bird until its demise.

Eyrie See *ayre*.

Falcon Traditionally the female peregrine, but nowadays used to denote other species of the larger long-wings.

Falconer The person who normally flies long-wings as opposed to the short-winged hawks.

Fall at mark, to To put quarry into cover, then alight on the ground beside it.

Feak To wipe the beak, usually on the perch or gauntlet, to cleanse it of particles of meat or other debris.

Fetch, to To reach the quarry and turn it, causing it to change its intended route.

Filanders Intestinal worms.

Flags The secondary wing feathers.

Fly on head, to To miss the quarry and check.

Foot, to To strike or clutch with the foot. A good footer is a hawk that catches her quarry well and holds it.

Fret marks Fine lines appearing across the webbing of feathers still in growth, said to be caused by shock or a period of time with no food, hence, hunger traces.

Frounce A growth in the mouth and throat of hawks, once fatal but now easily cured with modern drugs.

Full-summed After the moult when all new feathers have hardened off and have reached their full length.

Get in, to To reach the hawk as soon as possible after a kill.

Gleam The mucous sometimes thrown up after regurgitating a pellet or casting.

Gorge Fully fed, full crop, or to eat to repletion.

Hack The state of liberty which young hawks are allowed prior to training. The period of hack usually spans several weeks.

Hack back, to To carefully reintroduce a hawk back into its wild environment as opposed to simply setting it free.

Hack bells Large, heavy bells put on hawks at hack to prevent, or hinder them from preying for themselves.

Haggard An adult, wild-caught hawk. The term 'old hag' is said to be derived from this.

Halsband Called Jangaoli in the east, a neckband of leather or plaited silk placed like a collar around the neck with the end held in the hand, said by eastern falconers to give the hawk more impetus when leaving the fist. A device which has never found much favour with European falconers.

Hard-penned A hawk is said to be hard-penned, or full-summed when all the feathers are hard and no longer in the blood. See *Full-summed*.

High A term generally denoting that a hawk is overweight.

Hood The leather cap used to blindfold a hawk.

Hood off To remove the hood and slip the hawk at quarry.

Hood shy A hawk that bates at the sight of the hood, usually as a result of clumsy hooding by inexperienced falconers. The hawk thereafter dislikes the hood.

Hunger trace See *Fret marks*.

Imp, to To repair a broken or damaged feather by means of either a triangular needle or by a stitching process.

Inke An obsolete word meaning the neck of the quarry.

Intermewed A hawk that has moulted at least once in captivity.

Jack A male merlin.

Jangaoli See *halsband.*

Jerkin The male, or tiercel of the Gyr-falcon, the worlds largest falcon, occurring in the far north, ie Greenland, Iceland and Alaska. Ranging in colour from almost black to pure white.

Jesses Leather leg straps by which a hawk is held.

Jokin Sleeping (now obsolete).

Kecks See *croaks.*

Leash Long strip of leather, or braided nylon by which the hawk is tethered to the perch.

Lines, lunes, lewnes, loynes Now obsolete. Believed to be the jesses, or part of the jesses.

Long-winged hawks The true falcons, ie, species having long pointed wings, dark eyes, shortish tails and knotched or toothed beaks.

Lores, A naked, or semi-naked area of skin between the beak and the eyes of the bird.

Lure An artificial imitation of a bird (for falcons) or a rabbit (for Goshawks), to which the hawk is stooped or called for exercise, or to which it is recalled after an unsuccessful flight.

Mail The breast feathers of a hawk.

Make in To approach a hawk on the lure or quarry.

Make hawk An experienced hawk flown with an inexperienced hawk as a cast in order to encourage her to take a particular quarry.

Manning To tame a hawk by carriage on the gloved fist and to teach it to endure strange sights and sounds.

Mantle, to Spreading of the wings and tail, often in an attempt to hide the quarry from prying eyes. A habit more commonly seen in eyasses.

Mar-hawk To ruin, or mar a hawk through ineptitude or carelessness on the part of the falconer.

Mew To moult.

Mews Formerly a shed, or room where hawks were turned loose to moult. Nowadays any building where hawks are kept is normally referred to as the mews.

Musket A male Sparrowhawk.

Mutes The droppings, or excrement of hawks.

Nares The nostrils of a hawk.

Pannel Obsolete word for a hawk's stomach.

Pantas An old name for a disease of the respiratory tract.

Passage hawk A wild hawk in immature plumage caught on migration.

Pelt The dead body of any quarry killed by a hawk.

Petty singles The toes of a hawk.

Pitch The height which a falcon attains when waiting on.

Plume, to To pluck the quarry.

Put in, to To drive quarry into cover.

Put out, to To flush quarry out of cover.

Put over, to To pass food from the crop to the stomach using snake-like contractions of the neck.

Pounces The claws of a hawk.

Quarry The game flown at.

Rake away To abandon the intended flight and soar away downwind.

Rangle Small round pebbles, often administered overhand to a hawk in the process of being trained. These are believed to break up excess mucous and so aid enseaming.

Reclaim, to A term often used to mean the retraining of a hawk after the moult.

Red hawk Usually applied only to the peregrine, meaning the reddish-brown plumage of the first-year bird.

Ring up To rise to a height in spirals or circles, often using thermals to achieve this end.

Robin A male Hobby, one of the worlds smallest falcons. Rather like a miniature Peregrine, usually found in the more southern counties of its British range.

Rouse To raise and shake the feathers.

Rufter hood A plain and simple hood without a plume, used usually by hawk trappers.

Sails The wings of a hawk.

Sarcel The short outermost primary feather of the wing.

Seel, to The sewing together of the eyelids with silk thread, of a newly trapped hawk, a practice used only in Eastern countries.

Serve, to To flush the quarry from cover for the waiting hawk.

Sharp-set Hungry and keen.

Slice, Slicings Droppings or excrement of short-winged hawks, buzzards and eagles.

Slip To release the hawk from the fist at quarry.

Snite, to To sneeze.

Sock A type of jacket whereby a hawk may be restrained to prevent them damaging themselves, especially in transit to foreign countries.

Sore hawk A wild caught hawk in immature plumage, see *passage hawk.*

Stand, to take To remain perched in a tree or other vantage point after an unsuccessful flight, or from disobedience.

Stoop To dive from a height with closed wings after quarry or lure.

Strike the hood To open the braces of the hood in readiness to hood off at the moment quarry is sighted.

Swivel Two riveted metal hoops, designed to prevent the jesses and leash from becoming twisted.

Throw up, to To gain elevation, usually after a stoop.

Tiercel, tassel, tercel, tarsell Nowadays improperly used to denote a male hawk, properly it applies only to the male Peregrine.

Tiring A tough piece of meat given to a hawk to prolong the meal and keep her from boredom. Especially useful during early training.

Tower, to See *ring up*.

Train The tail of a hawk.

Truss, to To clutch and bind to the quarry in mid-air.

Tyrrit The old name for a swivel.

Turn tail, to To refuse the quarry in mid-flight.

Unreclaimed Wild.

Varvels Small flat silver rings, used in the old days in place of the more modern swivel. Often the owners name and coat of arms was engraved upon them.

Wait-on, to To circle above the falconers head, waiting for the quarry to be flushed.

Wake, to To man a hawk by keeping it awake. An old method of taming a hawk more quickly, but seldom used today.

Warble To spread the tail and stretch both wings over the back until they almost touch each other.

Washed meat Meat that has been soaked in water, so that much of the blood and its nutritive value has been washed out. Used by some for reducing the condition of hawks.

Weather, to To place a hawk out in the open on its perch.

Yarak An oriental term denoting that a hawk is keen and in flying condition.

Index